DATE DUE	

ANOREXIA
AND
BULIMIA

—Diseases and People—

ANOREXIA AND BULIMIA

Paul R. Robbins, Ph.D.

 Enslow Publishers, Inc.

40 Industrial Road	PO Box 38
Box 398	Aldershot
Berkeley Heights, NJ 07922	Hants GU12 6BP
USA	UK

http://www.enslow.com

This book is dedicated to Richard and Margit Cram

Library of Congress Cataloging-in-Publication Data

Robbins, Paul R. (Paul Richard)
    Anorexia and bulimia / Paul R. Robbins
        p. cm. — (Diseases and people)
    Includes bibliographical references and index.
    Summary: Explores the history of anorexia, bulimia, and binge eating,
discussing their symptoms, diagnosis, prevention, and treatment.
    ISBN 0-7660-1047-3
        1. Anorexia nervosa—Juvenile literature. 2. Bulimia—Juvenile
literature. [1. Eating disorders. 2. Anorexia nervosa. 3. Bulimia.]
    I. Title. II. Series.
    RC552.A5R62   1998
    616.85'26—dc21   97-34157
                                                          CIP
                                                          AC

Printed in the United States of America

10 9 8 7 6 5 4

Illustration Credits: Archive Photos, p. 48; Kelly Chin / *The Kansas City Star*, p. 41; © Corel Corporation, pp. 19, 38, 45, 61, 75, 84, 87; National Institutes of Health, p. 71; Quintessence Publishing Co., Inc. and Lance R. Hazelton, D. M. D., M. S. D., p. 51; Skjold Photographs, pp. 12, 28, 32, 64; U.S. Department of Agriculture, p. 100; Donald A. Williamson, p. 54.

Cover Illustration: © 1998 George White, Jr.

Contents

Acknowledgments

The author would like to thank Sharon Hauge, George Lane, Martha Weaver, and Larry Robbins for their contributions to the book. Grateful acknowledgment is made to the following for use of drawings and photographs: Donald A. Williamson, the *Kansas City Star*, Archive Photos, and Lance Hazelton. In addition, the author would like to thank Quintessence Publishing Company for permission to use materials from the article by L. Hazelton and M. Faine, "Diagnosis and Dental Management of Eating Disorder Patients," *International Journal of Prosthodontics*, January–February 1996.

ANOREXIA, BULIMIA, AND BINGE EATING DISORDER

What are they? Anorexia, bulimia, and binge eating disorder are three of the most common eating disorders. These disorders can have serious health consequences.

Who gets them? Anorexia and bulimia are much more likely to occur among women than men. Anorexia often begins during the teenage years. Binge eating disorder occurs about equally often among men and women.

How do you get them? The causes of these disorders are complex. Biological, psychological, and social factors all play a role. Eating disorders often begin with a diet to lose weight.

What are the symptoms? People with anorexia show substantial weight loss. Bulimia is less obvious because the purging routines that are part of the disorder are usually carried out in secret. People with binge eating disorder are usually overweight.

How are they treated? Severe anorexia is life-threatening, requiring hospitalization and careful refeeding. Bulimia can be treated by antidepressant medicines and by psychotherapy, particularly a form of therapy called "cognitive-behavioral therapy." The treatment of overweight caused by binge eating often requires a diet plan and psychotherapy.

How can they be prevented? Eating regular meals and a balanced diet is important. Rejecting the idea that a person must be very thin to be beautiful is essential.

Introduction

When Alma was fifteen years old, she was five feet, six inches tall and weighed 120 pounds. She was described as healthy and well developed. If Alma had looked at a chart in her doctor's office that listed desirable weights for different heights, she would have seen that her weight was fine. Then things began to change in Alma's life. Following her father's suggestion that she watch her weight, she began to restrict her food intake and went on a rigid diet. She also began a program of ferocious exercise that included tennis, swimming, and calisthenics. With this very restrictive diet and intensive exercise, she lost weight rapidly, becoming thinner and thinner. She reached the point where she looked like a walking skeleton, with every rib showing. Her face became hollow. Her skin developed a yellowish tint. To others she looked terrible. But Alma said she looked fine and that there was nothing wrong with her.[1]

Lisa was described as an isolated, lonely person. She felt "angry, frightened, and depressed." When things were not going well for her, she began to eat large quantities of sweets—"pounds of candy and cake at a time." Then she would experience feelings of guilt and self-disgust. She made herself vomit what she had eaten. Vomiting kept her weight from ballooning. Lisa kept these behavior patterns secret from others, but became increasingly depressed by what she was doing. Finally, after a suicide attempt, she was referred to treatment at an eating disorders clinic.[2]

In a psychiatric journal, a patient was identified only as "Case C." She was about thirty years old, well educated, intelligent, and a mother of two children. At times she would become very depressed, sitting almost motionless in her bathrobe, brooding. And then, like Lisa, she would begin to eat. Eating made her feel better. Once she started eating, it seemed as if there was no stopping. She ate everything in sight—sweets, pastry, bread, and more. She ate until everything that was available was gone. And then her depressed feelings returned and she became remorseful and promised herself never to do it again.[3]

These cases describe people who have eating disorders. Alma, who starved herself to an emaciated condition, has a disorder called anorexia nervosa. Lisa, who binged on food and then purged herself to keep her weight down, has a disorder called bulimia nervosa. Like Lisa, "Case C" binged on food, but did not purge herself. She has binge eating disorder.

All of these eating disorders can have serious physical and emotional consequences. Anorexia nervosa is especially dangerous. Many young people have died from medical complications of the disorder. The routines of vomiting or laxative use found in bulimia can have many undesirable effects on the body. Binge eating disorder often leads to obesity, the state of being greatly overweight.

Normal Eating Behavior

Eating disorders involve abnormal patterns of eating behavior. To better understand these patterns, we need to have some standard of what normal eating is. But setting a standard is not as easy as one might suppose. What is considered normal eating varies somewhat as a person moves from one part of the world to another and can change over the years. We might offer a definition that uses the height–weight charts found in a doctor's office. We might consider normal eating as that which leads to staying within the appropriate boundaries on the chart. But one can quickly see that some people might stay within these figures by dieting or by intentionally vomiting their food after overeating, as in bulimia.

What about dieting? How normal is that? In 1974, a survey found that three quarters of women college students surveyed had dieted in an effort to keep their weight down.[4] Later studies have continued to show that most women college students, as well as high school girls, have dieted.[5] If we can define "normal" as what most people do, it would appear that dieting among college women is perfectly normal. But is it really? Is it possible that these high figures are in part a response to society's pressure for women to be thin, a pressure that is strong in our own time but could change in future years?

Janet Polivy and C. Peter Herman, researchers who have studied eating behavior for many years, have offered a

Eating when you are hungry and stopping when you are full is considered normal eating.

definition of normal eating that avoids some of these complications. They wrote, "We define normal eating simply as eating that occurs in response to hunger cues and stops in response to satiety cues."[6] Satiety means feeling full. So if we look at it this way, normal eating means eating when you feel hungry and stopping when you feel full. Any practice that begins to diverge from this model would be a bit less normal.

But even now we have to be careful. If a religion teaches people to fast at certain times, the practice may be an unusual episode in their daily routines, but it is hardly abnormal. Jews are expected to fast on Yom Kippur, a day of prayer and atonement. During Ramadan, the ninth month of the Islamic calendar, Muslims are expected to fast until evening. Among American Indians in the Great Plains, young men went to lonely spots and fasted for several days in the hope of experiencing a revelation.[7] All of these examples of fasting are long-standing cultural traditions and are not indications of eating disorders. Fasting becomes abnormal when it becomes a routine part of daily life. This is what one sees in anorexia nervosa.

Culture and Eating

It is difficult to fully understand eating disorders without some understanding of the culture in which these disorders occur. The term *culture* comes from anthropology, the study of peoples throughout the world. Culture refers to the beliefs, values, traditions, and behavior patterns that most of the people in a society hold. The culture of a society is passed on from generation to generation and has a profound influence on what individuals think and do.

A very important part of any cultural tradition is the attitudes and behaviors relating to food and eating. Among the Bemba, a people who live in the African nation of Zambia, daily life is centered on food and drink. Throughout the day, conversation is focused on what the last meal was like and what the next meal will be.[8] In the United States most of us are much less preoccupied with food. We usually have many other things to think about, such as the demands of school or our jobs. Americans with eating disorders, however, may be more preoccupied with food than the Bemba; we shall see that for people with eating disorders, waking hours are filled with thoughts of food and food-related ideas and rituals.

How much we eat, what we eat, and whom we eat with are all influenced by the traditions of one's culture. During World War II, American pilots in the South Pacific went hungry rather than eat the food that was readily available—lizards, toads, and insects—because they had learned attitudes that made these foods seem disgusting.[9] It is clear that Polivy and Herman's view of what is normal eating—start when you are hungry and stop when you are full—can be altered by cultural traditions. You can probably think of circumstances in your own life where you may have been hungry but felt it would be inappropriate to begin eating. A simple example would be when guests are late for dinner. We can all think of more profound circumstances that could move people to behave differently from Polivy and Herman's model of normal eating.

Natural disasters, war, or famine can cause great changes in normal eating patterns. Grief and depression are psychological states that can diminish eating.

When we talk about an eating disorder, we move very far away from this model of normal eating. We are now talking about lifestyles in which thinking about food, weight gain and body image, and ritual behaviors relating to eating become a central focus in one's life. Eating is then no longer a matter of satisfying hunger pangs or a convenient opportunity to get together with family and friends to exchange news and conversation. Instead, it is a constant preoccupation linked to behavior patterns that often result in harm to the person with the disorder.

In this book we focus on the three eating disorders: anorexia nervosa (self-starvation), bulimia nervosa (binge eating followed by purging, fasting, or excessive exercise), and binge eating disorder (binge eating without purging or other compensating behaviors). In our discussion of binge eating, we shall discuss obesity—often a result of binge eating and a widespread problem in this country.

2

History of Eating Disorders

Scientists have studied anorexia for a longer period of time than either bulimia or binge eating disorder. However, each of these disorders has an interesting history that contributes to our understanding of the diseases.

Anorexia Nervosa

Two nineteenth-century physicians are given principal credit for identifying anorexia nervosa as a disorder and bringing it to the attention of the medical community. The first physician was a French neurologist, Charles Lasègue, who used the term *anorexia* in 1873. Lasègue believed the disorder was caused by emotional problems, such as conflicts between the anorexic patient and her parents.[1] The second physician, Sir William Gull, was well known in British medical circles and served as medical consultant to Queen Victoria. Gull presented case studies of anorexic girls, along with their photographs, to his medical colleagues and discussed how to diagnose and treat the condition.[2] Here are some excerpts from one of Gull's original cases:

> Miss A., age 17 . . . was brought to me on Jan. 17, 1866. Her emaciation was very great. It was stated that she had lost 33 lbs. in weight . . . complete anorexia for animal food, and almost complete anorexia for anything else. Abdomen shrunk and flat, collapsed . . . the condition was one of simple starvation. . . . Various remedies were prescribed . . . but no perceptible effect followed their administration. The diet also varied, but without any effect upon the appetite . . . the patient complained of no pain, but was restless and active. This was in fact a striking expression of the nervous state, for it seemed hardly possible that a body so wasted could undergo the exercise which seemed agreeable.[3]

Religious Fasting in Medieval Times

Reports of anorexic-like behavior go back centuries before Lasègue and Gull began to carefully define the disorder. Historian Joan Brumberg traced behavior patterns resembling anorexia to late medieval times—to the fourteenth century.[4] Like modern anorexic patients, some fourteenth-century women starved themselves into emaciated conditions. The reasons they did so were quite different, however, from what we observe now. Today the usual reasons offered for self-starvation relate to a perception of one's body size that one is too fat. The reasons for starving oneself in medieval times were based on religious beliefs.

In order to understand why these medieval women did what they did, it is important to recognize that the outlook on life during the medieval years was very different from what it is today. For many people who lived in those centuries, life was not only very hard but often very short. Science was in its infancy, public health measures that we take for granted (for example, purifying the water) did not exist, and infectious diseases could sweep through populations. In this rather bleak existence, people's thoughts often turned to the next world where they felt things had to be better. Many people became monks and nuns, turning their backs on the world to begin a life within the walls of monasteries and convents.

Some of these people went beyond renouncing the world. They attempted to make themselves more pure by acts of self-denial and self-punishment. Brumberg tells the story of a fourteenth-century woman, Catherine of Siena, who slept on a bed of thorny substances, scalded herself, and struck herself. In what sounds very much like anorexia, she ate only a handful of herbs each day. Sometimes she shoved twigs into her throat to bring back food she might have been forced to eat, which is similar to behavior we now see in patients with bulimia nervosa.[5]

Extreme fasting that was religiously motivated decreased as the medieval period ended. Starving oneself was less likely to be viewed as an act of piety. By the time of the Reformation—the religious movement of the sixteenth century that established the Protestant churches—such fasting was viewed as evidence of possible possession by demons.[6] If an anorexic

The reasons people starved themselves in medieval times were based on religious beliefs.

did not die from starvation, there was now the possibility of being burned as a witch.

Fasting Girls: A Medical Curiosity

If there had been supermarkets in England in the year 1807 with the kind of tabloid newspapers we see in these stores today, one might have read the following headline: "Sensational story of woman who survives without touching food." The woman, Ann Moore, was the latest in a succession of women who claimed to eat nothing (or next to nothing) and somehow survived. Ann Moore's story created interest not only in England, but in the United States as well. People wondered about women like Ann Moore: What kept them alive? Was it due to divine providence? Some people even speculated that these women were being fed invisible food by invisible fairies. Other people simply scoffed and said that the women were frauds. For Ann Moore, that certainly proved to be the case. She finally admitted that her mother had been slipping her food in subtle ways, such as kissing her and transferring food from between her lips. Moore made a tidy sum of money out of the charade, for she was more than willing to accept contributions from the many curious people who came to see her.[7]

Stories of fasting girls continued to surface on both sides of the Atlantic. In the 1880s, the mother of a twenty-year-old American girl signed a sworn statement that her daughter had not eaten anything in over six months except a tiny piece of watermelon and a piece of beefsteak the size of a caramel.[8] Promoters tried to get one fasting girl to appear in exhibitions.

Stories of fasting girls decreased as the nineteenth century closed. The work of Lasègue and Gull had convinced the medical profession that despite the occasional appearance of con artists like the Moore family, self-starvation was a serious medical problem that needed careful investigation. Physicians reported that young women were dying from anorexia nervosa and nobody was sure of the cause. As this grim description from a 1910 medical book testifies, anorexia could turn a healthy body into a pathetic, cadaver-like figure: "A young woman thus afflicted, her clothes scarcely hanging together on her anatomy, her pulse slow and slack, her temperature two degrees below the normal mean . . . her hair like that of a corpse dry and lusterless, her face and limbs ashy and cold, her hollow eyes the only vivid thing about her."[9]

The mid-nineteenth-century view of anorexia as a medical curiosity had given way to the serious search for causes and treatments. In our time, public awareness of anorexia has increased following the publication of autobiographies of those who have had the disorder, movies that dramatized the disorder, articles in popular magazines, and television interviews with people who have had eating disorders. One such television program took place in 1993 when Diane Sawyer interviewed actress Tracey Gold about her struggles with anorexia.[10] Gold had bouts of anorexia since the age of twelve and has been coping with the problem with the aid of a therapist and nutritionist. The word *anorexic*, which means "without appetite," has now become part of our vocabulary.

Bulimia Nervosa

Although bulimia nervosa was not firmly established as an eating disorder until the late 1970s, scholars have uncovered eating disorders that resemble bulimia in references dating back to earlier centuries. The ancient Romans were said to have used a vomitorium to relieve themselves after gorging food.[11] In 1743, an English medical dictionary described a condition called "true boulimus," which was characterized by preoccupation with food, overeating, and in some instances vomiting.[12] However, such historical references were quite scattered over the years and did not attract the sustained attention of the medical community.

In the late 1970s the situation changed. Reports of the disorder began to appear in medical journals. Shortly afterward, stories about bulimia appeared in popular magazines. Public interest in bulimia developed so rapidly that *Newsweek* labeled 1981 as "The Year of the Binge-Purge Syndrome."[13]

An interest in bulimia grew out of the research on anorexia. Investigators found that large numbers of patients they considered anorexic were engaging in binging and purging routines. The researchers were intrigued and referred to these patients as "vomiters," "vomiters and purgers," or "bulimics" to contrast them with the more traditional anorexic patients who were essentially starving themselves.

A number of different names were proposed for this newly recognized disorder of binging and purging, including "dysorexia," "bulimarexia," and "dietary chaos syndrome."[14]

Eventually researchers settled upon "bulimia nervosa." The word *bulimia* has a Greek origin meaning "ox hunger."

Binge Eating Disorder

Binge eating has been part of the human experience for a long time, but the recognition of binge eating disorder as a clinical disorder occurred only recently. Much of the credit for defining this disorder is given to Albert Stunkard, a psychiatrist who wrote an important paper about binge eating in 1959.[15] Binge eating as a behavior pattern probably dates to ancient history. The Romans had a reputation for eating to excess. During past centuries, some members of the British aristocracy often overstuffed themselves with meals that had one large course after another. Overindulging did not escape the American colonists, either. Benjamin Franklin noted that he had seen few people die of starvation but hundreds who died from eating and drinking.[16]

Many people who binge do not purge. Since it would be confusing to call such people bulimics, the term *binge eating disorder* came into being as a way to classify such behavior.

Prevalence of Eating Disorders Today

How many people have eating disorders in the United States? It is harder to answer this question than one might suspect. A researcher might try inquiring at doctors' offices and hospitals about patients with eating disorders. The problem with this approach is that many people with eating disorders tend to be secretive about what they do and many do not seek treatment. The statistics the researcher would obtain would therefore be lower than the true number of cases.

An alternative approach is to conduct interview surveys of households in a manner similar to census-taking or to give out questionnaires to groups of people such as classes of students. Using such techniques, researchers have carried out many studies to estimate the number of people with eating disorders. The results of these studies differ somewhat from one another, but the estimates are that anorexia is found in less than one percent of the population. Bulimia occurs more often, but the estimates are still around one percent. The estimates for binge eating disorder run around 3 to 4 percent.[17] Although these percentages are small, with the population of the United States now at more than 260 million, simple arithmetic tells us that millions of people have eating disorders.

How Many People Have Eating Disorders?

In addition to those who have serious cases of eating disorders, millions of other people have these tendencies in a less severe form. Many of these people will progress to unmistakable cases of eating disorders.

3

What Is Anorexia Nervosa?

When her anorexic behavior began, Claudia was five feet, two inches tall and weighed 105 pounds. She feels that it was her own self-doubts and her boyfriend's admiration of skinny thighs that started her on a diet that developed an unstoppable momentum. She lost 30 pounds in six months. She said that she was trying to maintain the weight of a ten-year-old. Claudia ate less and less, dividing her food into very small portions. Sometimes she carried her meal to her bedroom, then flushed it down the toilet. Her weight fell to 70 pounds. One day during a subway ride, a man looked at her and referred to her as a "walking skeleton." Claudia survived her bout with anorexia and eventually recovered her health. Many other anorexics are not as lucky.[1]

Anorexia nervosa is a disorder characterized by a large weight loss, a fear of weight gain, and faulty eating patterns. It is usually thought of as a disorder of young women, particularly girls in their teens. This perception is not far off the mark. There is a dramatic difference in the likelihood of men and women developing anorexia. In a 1993 statement on anorexia nervosa, the American Psychiatric Association observed that 90 to 95 percent of the cases are female.[2] In addition, anorexia very often begins during the teenage years. Although most anorexic patients are teenage girls or young women, some men as well as some older women also develop the problem.

Observers have been struck by the wasted, emaciated appearance of anorexics. Even though other people may say that the anorexic patient looks like a victim of starvation, the patient herself may insist that she is fat. This is puzzling and hard to understand. It is as if the patient is denying, even defying, reality.

Researchers have carried out experiments to study the distorted body image that anorexics have of their actual body size. One of the procedures involved the use of a color video camera. While the anorexic patient sat before the camera, the researcher captured a full frontal picture and stored it on the computer. The patient was then told that she would see a series of life-size pictures of herself that would be distorted, making her appear wider or thinner than she actually was. Each time her picture appeared, the patient was instructed to report whether it was too wide or too thin when compared with her actual size. The responses of the anorexic patients were compared with those of a group of college students who followed the same procedure and evaluated their own pictures. While the college students were pretty accurate in judging their body size, the anorexic patients overestimated their actual body size. They judged their bodies to be larger than they really were.[3]

Diagnosing Anorexia Nervosa

The American Psychiatric Association has set forth guidelines for diagnosing anorexia.[4] An important sign is the person's refusal to maintain body weight at anything close to what the charts tell us is normal for the person's age and height. If a person remains at 85 percent or less of normal weight, the person is within anorexic levels. Simple arithmetic gives us an illustration. If the chart tells us that a teenage girl should weigh at least 110 pounds and she is consistently under 93 pounds, her doctor might begin to wonder. If her doctor begins to inquire and finds that she has an intense fear of gaining weight and is preoccupied with thoughts about how her body looks, it would seem more and more like a case of anorexia. Further inquiries would probably reveal that the girl eats very little and has missed several menstrual cycles. Finally, the doctor might find that she denies she has a real problem.

These then are some of the classic signs of anorexia: marked underweight, fear of gaining weight, preoccupation with body image, restricted food intake, disruption of the menstrual cycle, and denial. And for many anorexics, we might add an exaggerated emphasis on exercise. Some people with anorexia exercise to the point of exhaustion.[5]

A doctor may need to ask the patient many questions to determine whether she has anorexia.

Medical Consequences of Anorexia Nervosa

The medical consequences of anorexia are severe and in many cases life-threatening. Most of these consequences are the result of starvation. The heart is affected and may no longer work at its highest capacity. The pulse and blood pressure fall to abnormally low levels. Abnormalities may show up on echocardiograms—records of the electrical activity of the heart. Studies of the effects of prolonged starvation show that the heart itself can shrink.[6]

The digestive system is another common casualty of anorexia. Patients report stomach pain and constipation. The bowel may become less active. The patient may feel full soon after starting to eat.[7]

Many anorexic patients have hypoglycemia—low levels of sugar in the blood. Women's menstrual cycles are disrupted. Anorexic patients may experience a feeling of being cold.

Bones of anorexic patients become thin. Not only is there bone loss, but the usual development of bone that occurs in adolescence may be impaired if the disorder begins during the teenage years. For some anorexic patients, bones are so thin that they may fracture easily.[8]

Anorexic patients often develop problems with their skin. The skin becomes dry and tends to crack. In some patients, hands and feet may take on a bluish tint, or the skin has a yellowish tone. This color may persist for years even when the patient has regained weight. The patient's toenails and fingernails may become brittle. Her hair may become thinned

29

and lose its luster. A fine type of hair, called lanugo hair, may grow on the patient's face and neck.[9]

Other problems that may occur with anorexia nervosa include mild anemia (reduction in the number of circulating red blood cells), swollen joints, and light-headedness. The patient may feel dizzy when standing up.[10] Some patients may complain of excessive thirst. There is also some evidence that the body's immune system may be affected, which may impair the body's ability to fight infections.[11]

Finally, we must mention something that sounds bizarre enough to be out of a Hollywood horror film, and that is a shrinking brain. It would be reassuring if we were talking about some science-fiction story complete with mad scientists and strange machines that throw out pulsating electrical charges. Unfortunately, it can really happen in anorexia, as the National Institute of Mental Health (NIMH) notes in its pamphlet "Eating Disorders": "In some patients, the brain shrinks, causing personality changes."[12]

Evidence of brain abnormalities was recently reported in a study carried out in Australia. Forty-six hospitalized patients with anorexia nervosa were compared with forty-one normal-weight controls, using magnetic resonance imaging (MRI) pictures of the brain. A significant number of the anorexic group showed brain abnormalities.[13] If you look at a drawing of the brain, you will see fissures (depressions). These fissures are called sulci. The brain images of some of the anorexic patients showed dilations (widening) of these fissures.

Survival Rates in Anorexia

About 10 to 15 percent of those afflicted with anorexia will die as a result of their condition. Many patients who survive will not make a full recovery.[14] Some symptoms may

The Australian team examined the performance of the anorexic patients on tests measuring attention, memory, and visual-spatial abilities. The anorexic patients did not do as well as the people in the control group. Was their relatively poor performance the result of brain changes? No one can say at this point.

This is a long, unhappy list of problems. Of all the problems on the list, the damage to the heart is probably the main reason for the large number of deaths of anorexic people. These deaths may occur suddenly. The longer the anorexia nervosa is untreated, the worse the situation is likely to become.

Anorexia Nervosa and the Family

In the 1870s Charles Lasègue proposed that emotional problems caused by conflicts within the family played a role in the development of anorexia nervosa. In recent times therapists who have worked with anorexics have echoed this theme. Mothers of anorexic patients have been described as

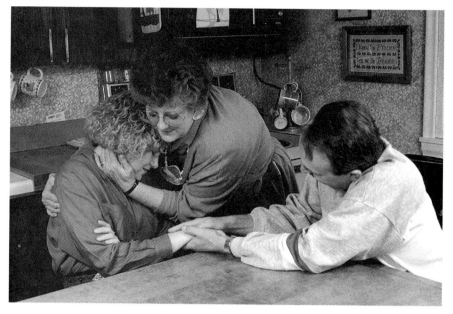

Many individuals with eating disorders have troubled home lives.

anxious, overprotective, perfectionistic, and fearful of separating from their children. Fathers are described as moody, withdrawn, and passive.[15] The anorexic patient has been viewed as a person who has difficulty separating from the family and developing her own identity. Families of anorexic patients may have trouble dealing with conflict.[16]

While research to date has been too limited to fully confirm these observations, studies indicate that many families of anorexics are troubled. Parents of anorexics tend to have psychological difficulties.[17] Both anorexic patients and their mothers have described their family as having difficulties in communicating.[18] Anorexic patients seem more likely to view their parents as "blaming, rejecting, and neglectful toward them" than is the case for normal controls.[19]

There may be a link between anorexia and a history of sexual assault. In household surveys from two sites—one in California and one in North Carolina—it was found that people who reported having been a victim of a sexual assault were more likely to report symptoms of anorexia.[20] There are reports suggesting that some of this trauma was inflicted in the home.[21]

In her book *The Golden Cage*, Hilde Bruch took the position that the development of anorexia was so closely linked to abnormal patterns of family interaction that these problems would have to be resolved if the anorexic person was to be successfully treated.

She also pointed out that the patient's family may not admit that these problems exist. Bruch described the case of Celia, who weighed in the low 70s and had to be fed intravenously. Investigations into her family situation yielded denials that there were any problems. Her mother stated that there had never been dissatisfactions in her marriage. She seemed angry that anyone would look for problems in the family.[22] It turned out that her relationship with her husband was almost childlike and characterized by extreme dependency.

Anorexic behavior itself may act to deepen conflicts and strains with the parents. Therapist Nancy Kolodny described a sixteen-year-old, Melinda P., who had anorexic and bulimic symptoms for two years. The more she advanced into her eating disorder, the less she cared about other things. She didn't talk much to her parents before the onset of these disorders, and after the disorder began she said, "I cut them out of my life completely."[23] Another of Kolodny's patients, a sixteen-year-old girl name Felicity, became furious with her parents when they tried to persuade her to go to a therapist. She felt that they were interfering with her plans to become anorexic thin. Her defiant comment was, "I'll show them—I'll get there."[24]

Although poor family relationships do play a role in the development of anorexia nervosa, one should be cautious about pushing the argument too far. There are vast numbers of families with serious interpersonal problems but no cases of anorexia. Conflicted family environments are fertile soil for the development of many problems in children, and anorexia is but one of them. It is true that in families where one

Serotonin and Changes in the Brain

One of the biological factors involved in anorexia is the neurotransmitter serotonin. Serotonin is a chemical that is used in transmitting signals in the brain. For many patients with anorexia, serotonin activity is abnormal.[25] The same is true for bulimia.

member develops anorexia, there is an increased likelihood that a second member of the family will also develop the problem. About 3 to 10 percent of sisters of patients may develop the disorder.[26] While that is a much larger figure than we find in the general population, it still means that 90 percent or more of the sisters do not develop the disorder. Clearly the family environment is only one of the factors in anorexia nervosa. There are other social, psychological, and biological factors involved.

Psychological Patterns in Anorexia Nervosa

People who have worked with anorexic patients have observed a number of psychological patterns that seem to characterize many anorexics. These patterns include a psychological drive for thinness, perfectionistic tendencies, and a fear of becoming mature. Researchers have developed a set of psychological scales to measure these three patterns and have included them in a questionnaire-like measure called the Eating Disorder Inventory. When the inventory was given to anorexic patients and their responses were compared with those of young people without eating disorders, anorexics scored higher on all three of these patterns.[27]

For most anorexics, the drive for thinness probably has its roots in our culture's view that to be slim is highly desirable. To be thin is said to be beautiful and to be beautiful is to be popular. Certainly, attractive people have advantages. When these ideas are accepted by an individual, they can be strongly motivating. The NIMH pamphlet "Eating Disorders" describes the case of Deborah: "Like many teenage girls, she was interested in boys but concerned that she wasn't pretty enough to get their attention. When her father jokingly remarked that she would never get a date if she didn't take off some weight, she took him seriously and began to diet relentlessly."[28] In time, Deborah was diagnosed with anorexia nervosa.

The equation in the thought process of many people that thinness = beauty = popularity has a flip side to it. Fat is viewed as unattractive, food causes fat, and therefore food should be avoided.

The theory that anorexic behavior is a response to a fear of growing up involves more complex psychological reasoning than the drive-for-thinness explanation. It has been observed that anorexia tends to appear when young people are faced with changes or new demands in their lives. An example would be the body changes that occur during adolescence. If a girl has fears about developing into an adult, what better way to prevent this than by refusing to eat? Bruch said that it was possible to describe anorexia as an effort to make time stand still.[29] The motivation was not to grow up but to return to childhood size and status. While this theory is intriguing, there needs to be a good deal more evidence set forth for it to be convincing.

If a young person is motivated to become thin, a perfectionistic personality style would certainly help get her there. Perfectionistic people hold standards that are nearly impossible to reach, and they have little tolerance for errors in themselves or others. We can see elements of perfectionism in many anorexics with their relentless exercise, calorie counting, and extreme standard of what thinness means. There is also an element of perfectionism, having almost an obsessive quality, in the rituals some anorexics go through when they eat. One such ritual was described as follows: The person cuts each piece of meat into four equal pieces. Then she eats only three of these, being sure that the fork does not touch her lips. Each chunk is chewed precisely twelve times.[30] It should be stressed that perfectionism is a characteristic of eating-disordered individuals and relates to their lives in general—not just to food, eating, and weight.

Sustaining Anorexic Behavior

What sustains anorexic behavior? Imagine that a fifteen-year-old girl went on an ultrastrict diet and reduced her weight from 115 pounds to 80 pounds. How would her parents and friends react? Chances are that her parents would put pressure on her to start eating again and regain some weight. Yet many anorexics resist such pressure; they continue their extreme food restriction. What is it that keeps the behavior pattern going?

One possibility is that some of the reinforcement that sustains anorexic behavior comes from the added attention the patient receives from the family. She is now the center of a family struggle and may find some satisfaction, consciously or unconsciously, in this role. It seems likely, however, that much of the reinforcement for anorexic behavior comes from within.

Many anorexics are overly concerned with exercise. Some exercise to the point of exhaustion.

There are few people patting the young woman on the back for becoming bone thin. Some of this reinforcement probably stems from inner convictions that her behavior is right for her—that it is sensible no matter what everyone else says. It has been reported that anorexic girls often looked in the mirror, examining themselves and taking pride in every bone that showed. Their response to criticism was that they looked just fine, the way they want to look.[31] Indeed, anorexic patients are generally pleased with the way their bodies look.[32]

Mental health professionals sometimes encounter people, such as paranoid individuals, who are convinced that "someone is out to get them." They have fixed ideas that are not supported by reality. Anorexics, too, may have fixed ideas about their body images, but otherwise are not much like these clearly mentally ill people. We do know that when many normal people make a decision to pursue a certain course of action, they will tend to develop belief systems that support that action. For example, if a person chooses a certain college, then he or she will learn more and more positive things about that college—the quality of the professors, the beauty of the campus, the range of student activities—all of which will tend to support the original decision to go there. This process of beliefs becoming closer to behavior is what psychologists call "reducing cognitive dissonance." Something like this may be happening in anorexics. Whatever the case, the process is happening in an extreme way, decreasing willingness to consider other points of view.

Some researchers have suggested an alternative explanation about what sustains anorexic behaviors. They believe that the process of starvation releases chemicals in the body called opioids—naturally produced substances that create a psychological high, a feeling of elation. In this view the anorexic continues to starve herself because starvation releases these opioids, which makes her feel good.[33]

Athletics and Anorexia

There have been publicized cases of young women athletes who have developed eating disorders while trying to keep their weight down. An outstanding gymnast, Christy Henrich, died from complications of anorexia at age twenty-two. From early childhood, Henrich had trained seven hours a day to make herself a world-class athlete. After competing in Europe, an official told her she needed to lose weight to make the Olympic team. She began to lose weight. This desire to be thinner probably led to her anorexia. At one point during the disorder, her weight dropped to 47 pounds.[34] The much admired ballerina Gelsey Kirkland also developed anorexia. Her mentor had told her to ignore pain and eat nothing.[35] For women athletes in gymnastics and figure skating, the pressure to be thin can be intense and has raised the concern of women's athletic associations. At a 1995 forum in Canada, which included members of the Canadian Gymnastics Federation and Figure Skating Associations, the need was voiced to educate athletes about nutrition and maintaining a proper weight for their type of body and activity.[36]

Gymnast Christy Henrich suffered from anorexia and at one point weighted only 47 pounds. She died at the age of twenty-two.

While high-profile cases of elite women athletes with eating disorders have been reported in the news, it is unclear how widespread these problems are among less elite women athletes. A study of 200 college-level gymnasts found that while the rate of clear-cut eating disorders was not unusually high, more than half of the women did things like unnecessary dieting, fasting, and excess exercising to burn calories.[37]

Even in track competition, which does not emphasize thinness like gymnastics, there are reports of women with eating disorders. A study of women track-and-field athletes in Australia found that the athletes who had experienced stress fractures scored higher on a test indicating the presence of eating disorders. The women with fractures were more likely to restrict their food intake, which seemed to increase vulnerability to bone breakage.[38] Perhaps the thinking goes something like this: "If I weigh less, maybe I can run faster." This may be true up to a point, but pushing the point too hard opens the door to eating disorders and bodily harm.

4

What Is Bulimia Nervosa?

Bulimia nervosa is an eating disorder that afflicts more people than anorexia nervosa. Unlike anorexia, bulimia is characterized by compulsive overeating and is usually followed by self-induced vomiting or laxative or diuretic abuse. The bulimic often feels guilty and depressed after an episode. Like anorexia, bulimia is a disorder that women are much more likely to experience than men. Bulimia may affect the nurse who lives across the street, the college student who lives around the corner, or a world-class athlete like Zina Garrison-Jackson.

Garrison-Jackson was one of the top tennis players in the world. Her bulimic symptoms began after her mother's death. The loss hit her very hard. She began to eat constantly, stuffing herself with junk food. Then she would feel guilty and throw up. In time, her eating habits robbed her of her strength. In one tennis match, she felt too weak to compete. She began to feel badly about herself. Recognizing that she needed help, she went into therapy, which helped her cope with her eating disorder. Now she is careful to eat a balanced diet to help prevent further episodes of bulimia.[1]

Bulimia often develops in the late teens or early twenties. If left untreated, the disorder can persist for many years. Bulimic patients are often well educated and typically come from middle-class backgrounds. A study carried out in the Netherlands indicates that bulimia is more likely to occur in cities than in rural areas.[2]

Diagnosing Bulimia Nervosa

Bulimia is a condition that is characterized by binging and purging. The word *binge* means to consume, usually in a short time, very large amounts of food or alcoholic drinks. For binge drinking, there are slang terms such as *benders* or *blasts*. For binge eating, one hears more unflattering terms such as *gobbling up* or *pigging out*.

Binging is something many of us do at times. The classic American example of overindulging in food is Thanksgiving dinner. The Thanksgiving meal may have a leisurely rather than a hurried pace. Still, picture in your mind that attractively set Thanksgiving dinner table with turkey, stuffing, cranberry sauce, candied sweet potatoes, hot rolls, and pumpkin pie. To most people, it's irresistible. And besides, there is a license to indulge that day. It's a feast and that is exactly what most of us do. We fill ourselves to the brim.

The typical American will overindulge in food on Thanksgiving.

The unwritten rules of our society give us permission to indulge on occasions such as Thanksgiving, but not as an everyday occurrence. The person with bulimia, however, gorges food regularly. It is somewhat similar to Lewis Carroll's tale, *Through the Looking-Glass,* in which presents are given for "unbirthdays" as well as for birthdays.

How often does a person have to binge and purge to be

diagnosed as a full-fledged bulimic? The American Psychiatric Association suggests on the average of twice a week for a three-month period.[3] Some people purge even more frequently, often several times a day.

Binge-Purge Cycle

People who are bulimic may "prep" themselves for bulimia by missing regular meals. In a study, bulimic patients were asked to monitor their eating. The bulimics reported that they ate fewer meals than a group of nonbulimics.[4] On the days that they binged, the bulimic patients ate relatively little in the hours before binge eating. However, they did not report increased hunger before binging. The bulimic patients were usually at home, often alone, when they binged. They often reported that they were in negative moods. Snacks and desserts were their favorite foods. Some of the bulimic patients consumed over 2,000 calories during a binge episode.[5]

The consequences of regular overeating are clear enough. The body will begin to expand. It might not be so bad if we could grow taller, but after the growth period is over, usually in one's teens, it doesn't work that way. We just get wider and thicker. Interestingly, as we shall see, many bulimics are terribly concerned about fat. They may try exercising vigorously, fasting, or using diet pills. What many of them end up doing is trying to rid their body of excess calories by vomiting or by using laxatives, enemas, or diuretics. Laxatives are familiar, heavily advertised products that are sold over-the-counter in pharmacies, supermarkets, and convenience stores. The makers of these products note on the packages that continued use of these medicines can lead to problems such as dependency. And as we shall see, that is exactly what happens to many bulimics. Diuretics may be less familiar than laxatives. These drugs have important medical uses, especially in the treatment of high blood pressure. Diuretics eliminate fluid from the body, which can have a temporary effect on weight. But in this process, diuretics eliminate important chemicals from the body such as potassium, which can pose a health risk. Diuretics are not effective drugs for weight control.

Some people with bulimia induce vomiting by sticking their fingers into their throats, which recalls the fourteenth-century story of Catherine of Siena. Other people have used a spoon or a toothbrush to induce vomiting. Some people are able to vomit spontaneously by turning their necks. Bulimics have also used chemical agents such as soap solutions.[6] Perhaps most dangerous is the use of ipecac syrup, which is used by physicians to induce vomiting in situations like drug overdoses. Ipecac syrup stays in the body for a long time. Repeated use can result in heart disturbances, and can be fatal. The singer Karen Carpenter may have died from the toxic effects of this drug.[7] Karen Carpenter had a very successful career, performing with her brother, Richard. The Carpenters sold millions of records and won Grammy awards. Karen struggled with eating disorders. She was thirty-two years old when she died.

Some people who binge on food may not plan to vomit; vomiting can happen as a reaction to excessive eating. There is

Karen Carpenter suffered with eating disorders and was thirty-two when she died.

an account of a patient who ate so much food in the afternoons and evenings that it could only be described as "unbelievable." She ate in succession three to four meals of three to four courses each. In addition, she ate pounds of cookies, chocolate, and other sweets. She reached a point where she could hardly breathe. Severe abdominal pains set in and she began vomiting.[8]

Medical Consequences of Bulimia

The medical complications of bulimia are much less likely to be life-threatening than those of anorexia, where the person's weight may become dangerously low. Nonetheless, bulimia can cause difficulties in various systems of the body. Depletion of body fluids through vomiting and through the use of laxatives and diuretics can change the chemical balances that are essential in regulating our bodies. The loss of potassium can be very serious. With inadequate levels of potassium, the patient may complain of muscular weakness. He or she may experience disturbances in heart rhythms. There is a possibility of sudden death.[9] When physicians prescribe diuretics for blood pressure, they may routinely monitor the patient's blood to make sure that the chemical balance remains normal. The bulimic who loses potassium through vomiting, laxative abuse, and the use of diuretics may not have this protection.

In many bulimic patients the salivary glands are swollen, which can cause the face to look puffy. It is not certain why this occurs. Several explanations have been offered by researchers, including the regurgitation of acid from the stomach. Swelling of the glands may begin a few days after a binging episode.[10]

The esophagus—the passage that leads from the mouth to the stomach—can be damaged by repeated vomiting. Ulcers of the esophagus may develop. The patient may complain of a sore throat or of indigestion. A rare worst-case scenario is that the esophagus may rupture.[11]

The continual use of laxatives can cause diarrhea. Regular use of laxatives can reduce the ability of the bowel to function. Dependency on laxatives may occur. The problem can become severe. The bowel becomes unresponsive. When a bulimic quits the laxative routine, it may take weeks to restore normal bowel functions.[12]

Dental problems are very common consequences of bulimia. Constant vomiting fills the mouth with stomach acids, which erode tooth enamel. Dental cavities are frequent.[13] Lance Hazelton and Mary Faine, who teach restorative dentistry at the University of Washington, noted that bulimic activity may produce distinctive symptoms in the mouth. There may be erosion of the front teeth, irritations of the mucous membranes, dryness of the mouth, and scaling of the surface of the lips and corners of the mouth. In addition, the patients' teeth may be sensitive to heat and cold. Continual purging makes dental restoration difficult because the teeth around the restorations are easily eroded. With some restorations the cement deteriorates and teeth are destroyed.[14]

A twenty-eight-year-old woman had a history of anorexia as well as of vomiting. Her height was five feet, nine inches, yet she weighed only 88 pounds. She had a history of alcohol and drug abuse, childhood sexual abuse, and a broken family. The woman was described as dependent on her mother yet resentful of her, blaming her mother for her condition. She attributed her inability to gain weight to the condition of her teeth. Dental examination revealed that almost all of her teeth were eroded. A quick look at a photograph of her upper front teeth might leave one with the impression that these teeth had been filed away, leaving concave surfaces. It took months of restorative dentistry to give her teeth a pleasing, normal appearance.[15]

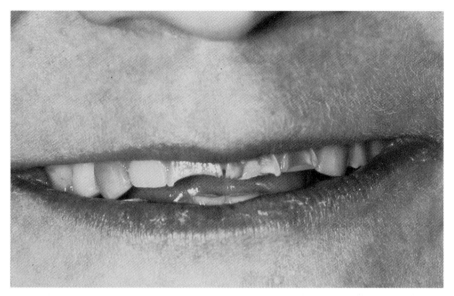

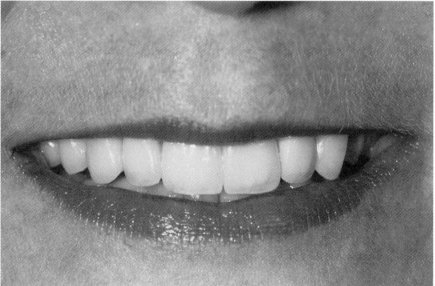

After months of dental work, a bulimic patient's teeth were transformed from the ones on the top to those on the bottom. The erosion had been caused by her bulimic activity.

Bulimia Nervosa and the Family

As is true for anorexia, research on the family relationships of bulimic patients is still somewhat limited. Researchers have reported that bulimic patients view their families as being less cohesive than do women without eating disorders. By "cohesive" we mean how well the family functions together as a unit. Bulimic families are also described as more conflicted and less supportive.[16] Bulimic patients see their parents as "blaming, rejecting, and neglectful toward them" and as not being nurturant.[17] In addition, bulimics more often describe their parents as depressed, having alcohol abuse problems, and having made a suicide attempt than do a comparison group of women.[18] Finally, bulimic patients are more likely to report having been sexually abused as children, a pattern noted in the case of the twenty-eight-year-old woman previously reported.

Psychological Studies of Bulimics' Body Image

Perhaps the best way to begin to understand bulimia is to examine the way many bulimics think about their bodies. Researchers have observed that bulimics were preoccupied with their weight and body size. Many bulimics have a marked fear of becoming fat and a belief that they are fat when they are not. They have convinced themselves that they are overweight. Many bulimics have a distorted idea of what they ought to weigh. Not only do they wish to be more slender than they are, they want to be at a weight below what is considered the minimum for their height. They have an anorexic-like wish.

A technique that has been used to demonstrate what bulimics think is a desirable body shape for themselves is to present them with a series of sketches of bodies ranging from very thin to very heavy and ask them for their evaluations. A research team led by Donald Williamson presented bulimic university students with nine such drawings and asked them to first "select the card that most accurately depicts your current body size, as you perceive it to be." Following this, the students were asked to "select the card that most accurately depicts the body size that you would most prefer."[19]

The findings are revealing. Students with bulimia saw themselves as larger than a group of students that served as controls—despite the fact that the bulimics and controls had been matched for both height and weight. The average weights of the two groups were almost identical. In regard to the body shape that was desired, the bulimics chose a smaller body size than the control group did. Bulimics saw themselves as "larger than their matched normal counterparts and wished to be much smaller."

Rituals and Preoccupations

Many bulimic patients begin their binging in a ritualistic fashion. Some rituals include using specific foods that might later help induce vomiting. Other rituals involve the use of foods that are distinctive in color or texture, on the theory that

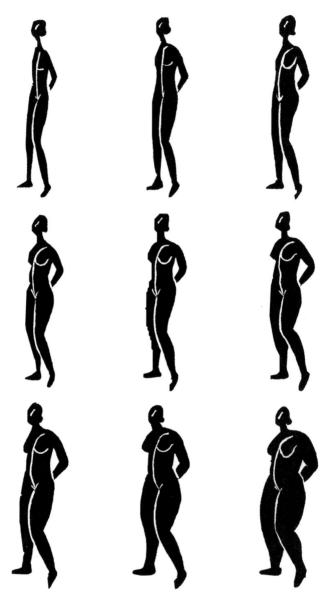

Bulimic students were asked to choose which image looked most like their body. The bulimic students saw themselves as larger than a control group of nonbulimic students that was matched for height and weight.

when the person sees the remains of this vomited food, she will know that she had been successful in purging herself.[20]

Many bulimics are very preoccupied with thoughts about food, weight gain, and the rituals they have adopted to prevent weight gain. One study found that bulimic patients averaged over three hours a day in thinking about food and weight gain and spent close to another two hours in purging rituals.[21] For these patients, a large part of every day was dedicated to the eating disorder. For some patients, preoccupation with food and weight gain becomes nearly intolerable. Some patients reported that they had less than three hours a day in which they felt completely free of these preoccupations—and for a few, the preoccupation with food and weight gain was continuous. Some patients said that these thinking patterns interfered with their lives. They might try to resist the thoughts—to put them out of mind—but the effort was unsuccessful. They felt that they had little control over their thoughts.

Obsessive-Compulsive Behaviors

You can see the obsessive quality in the daily life of these bulimic patients. Many cannot rid themselves of thoughts related to food and weight. Such thoughts fill their minds. Tension develops and increases, and the act of purging that follows may give them temporary relief. There is a lot in common between this pattern and the behavior of patients with a diagnosis of obsessive-compulsive disorder. The classic obsessive-compulsive case is a person who is obsessed with thoughts of uncleanliness and spends much time each day washing his or her hands. Hand washing may temporarily relieve the tension aroused by the thoughts relating to uncleanliness. It has been proposed that bulimia is similar to obsessive-compulsive disorder in that binging arouses anxiety and purging reduces that anxiety, much the same as hand-washing rituals function for the classic obsessive-compulsive patient.[22] Research findings seem to support this view. In studies of bulimics, subjective reports of anxiety increase after binging and decrease after purging.

Depression

Many people with bulimia are depressed. When people are depressed, they often feel sad or blue. They may not sleep well, their energy level is often low, and they tend to lose interest in the things they usually enjoy doing. There are a dozen separate studies linking depression and bulimia.[23] Many people with bulimia have attempted suicide. The fact that so many bulimics are depressed has led some researchers to question whether bulimia is really a separate disorder or merely another form of depression.[24]

Some bulimic patients experience periods not only of depression but also of hyperexcitement called mania. Their mood may be euphoric, and they may engage in activities at a frantic pace. The alternation between depressed states and periods of manic excitement is called bipolar disorder. About 12 percent of bulimic patients have a history of bipolar disorder.[25]

Depression, Self-Esteem, and Bulimia

Between 30 percent and 70 percent of bulimics are currently experiencing depression or have been depressed.[26] These figures are much higher than those for the general population. On psychological measures of self-esteem, bulimic women tend to score lower than women without eating disorders.[27]

Mrs. A. is an example of a patient with bulimia and bipolar disorder. She is a thirty-five-year-old woman who had been bulimic for twenty-two years. She binged on high-calorie foods as often as four times a week. Binging was most likely to occur when she was angry or felt rejected. Sometimes she purged after binging; sometimes she ate little between binges. Mrs. A. showed typical signs of depression. In addition to having a depressed mood, her energy was low, her concentration was poor, and she slept poorly.

Mrs. A. was given an antidepressant medicine that made her feel a lot better, but her bulimia persisted. Then one day she came into her eating disorders clinic in a euphoric mood. She reported she did not need to eat or sleep. She had gone on a buying spree. Her mood had cycled from depressed to manic. Lithium, a drug effective in controlling mania, was prescribed. Within a few days, she stopped binging. When she was angry or felt rejected, she thought about food, but did not binge.[28]

Perfectionism

As is the case for anorexia, many people with bulimia have perfectionistic tendencies. One can see elements of this in the desire to have a body size that is unrealistically thin. Some observers have noted that bulimia seems to occur more often in high achievers such as female students in medicine, law, and business.[29] In a study relating perfectionism and eating disorders in college women, bulimic tendencies were found to be related to the need to appear perfect. These women wanted to look good in the eyes of others.[30] This study suggests that many bulimic women may be purging themselves not so much to meet their own standards as to meet the standards of others.

Recovery in Bulimics

Studies of the long-term outcome of bulimia five to ten years following the presentation of the disorder indicated that about half the patients had fully recovered. Many of the remaining patients, however, were still clearly bulimic.[31]

5

What Is Binge Eating Disorder?

Binging on food repeatedly without the kind of purging rituals used by bulimics or without intensive exercise will usually lead to being overweight. Interestingly, binge eating often occurs during attempts to diet. What happens is that some people try to control their weight with dieting, slip somewhere along the line, throw in the towel, and end up with unrestrained binging. The intention is to be slim, but the result is just the opposite. Dieting followed by binge eating is usually self-defeating.

During World War II, conscientious objectors who would not fight in the war agreed to serve as subjects in an experiment to study the effects of starvation. They were put on a very low-calorie diet that reduced their weight to less than 75 percent of their initial weight. When normal quantities of food were finally made available, they gorged themselves.

Binge Eating in Men and Women

Unlike anorexia and bulimia, which occur much more often in women than in men, binge eating disorder occurs about equally often in men and women.[1]

Even after they regained their old weights, they continued "to binge, gorging at meals to the limit of their physical capacity."[2] These men were not known to be binge eaters before the experiment began. The use of extreme diets to lose weight had unintended consequences.

Diagnosing Binge Eating Disorder

The American Psychiatric Association has set forth tentative guidelines for diagnosing binge eating disorder. The guidelines stress the importance of recurrent episodes of binge eating in making a diagnosis. Some signs of binge eating disorder are

- Episodes of binge eating (consuming in a given period a quantity of food that is clearly larger than what most people would eat—along with a feeling of being unable to control one's eating behavior during that time) that occurs on the average of twice a week or more.

- Binging that extends over a period of six months.

- Eating until uncomfortably full.

- Eating large amounts of food when not feeling hungry.

- Eating alone because of embarrassment that one is eating too much.

- Psychological distress following binging.[3]

As is true for bulimics, foods used in binging include snacks and desserts, such as salty snack foods, sweets, cookies, pastries, and ice cream. Binges often are completed within the hour, though sometimes they may last for hours. Abdominal

Cakes, cookies, candies, and salty snacks are favorite foods for binging.

pains will often set in, putting an end to the binging episode. The person has eaten to the point of feeling sick.

Medical Consequences of Binge Eating

The major medical consequences of continual binge eating are the ones that come with being overweight. These medical problems tend to become worse as the person becomes markedly overweight and is clearly obese. The signs of obesity are pronounced body weight and masses of fatty tissue. In determining whether a person is obese, physicians may make use of a formula that gives a figure called the body mass index.[4] Another method is to use the height–weight chart. Some researchers have suggested that a weight that is 20 percent above the upper limit of weight listed on the chart may be taken as obesity.[5] A figure of 20 percent would be

---

Body Mass Index

The formula for body mass index is body weight in kilograms divided by the height in meters squared. An index of under 25 is considered desirable. For example, a woman who weighs 55 kilograms (121 pounds) and is 1.5 meters (5 feet) tall has a body mass index of 24.4:

$$\frac{55 \ kg}{(1.5 \ m)^2} = 24.4$$

---

considered mild obesity. The greater the excess over the listed weight, the greater the obesity.

People who are obese are more likely than people of normal weight to have a variety of medical problems. These problems may shorten the life of the person. Obese persons have higher death rates from many diseases (for example, heart attacks), from surgery, and from accidents. Other problems that may occur are lower back pain and large calluses on the feet and heels. Skin disorders may result when sweat gets trapped in the thick folds of skin, promoting the growth of bacteria.[6]

It should be stated that not every binge eater is obese and not every obese person is a binge eater. However, the two often go hand in hand. Studies suggest that about one third of obese patients seeking treatment engage in binge eating.[7]

Psychiatric Disorders Observed in Binge Eating Disorder

People who are mildly obese do not differ very much from people of normal weight in the likelihood of experiencing psychiatric problems. However, severely obese people have higher rates of psychiatric disorders such as depression and anxiety. Among obese people, those who practice binge eating are much more likely to have experienced a psychiatric disorder such as depression than are obese people who are not binge eaters. In research reported by Susan Yanovski and her colleagues, it was found that about half (51 percent) of the obese binge eaters they studied suffered from a major

Any feelings of stress or personal failure can bring on an episode of binge eating.

depression.[8] This compares with 14 percent for obese nonbinge eaters.

Psychological Explanations for Binging Behaviors

There is no simple explanation for why some people binge on food and others not only binge but purge. While researchers have offered good ideas about why people do these things, these ideas should be considered theories rather than clearly established facts. Like most theories, they are tentative. As more information becomes available about binge eating and purging, these theories are likely to change. Here is one line of explanation that has been offered as a way of better understanding both binge eating and purging:[9]

(1) Some people are predisposed to binging on food because of their personalities and previous experiences. Risk factors include low self-esteem, a tendency to be impulsive, and exposure to trauma such as childhood sexual abuse.

(2) Feelings of stress can bring on a binge eating episode. Any sense of personal failure or interpersonal unpleasantness could be a trigger for binge eating. The act of binging temporarily reduces the tension.

(3) Binging itself, however, can produce new tensions. Binging deepens feelings that one is not in control, promotes feelings of guilt and disgust, and deepens concerns about gaining weight.

(4) Purging may be used as a means to diminish or relieve the uncomfortable feelings brought on by binging. However, relief is only temporary.

(5) Dieting may be instituted as a way to stop weight gain. But dieting often leads to craving for food, renewed binging, and a repetition of the cycle. Constant repetition of this self-defeating behavior pattern can only deepen the feeling that one is out of control. In one study, 70 percent of the people studied experienced suicidal thoughts after binge-purge episodes.[10]

This model of binge eating assumes that tension or stress promotes overeating. Is this actually the case? A review of research indicates the question is not yet settled.[11] Some evidence that supports the idea comes from a study I carried out with Roland Tanck. Eighty college students, about equally split between men and women, were first asked about feelings of tension or anxiety they had been experiencing. Then, they were asked, "How do you cope with feelings of tension or anxiety when they arise? What things do you do to diminish or relieve these feelings?" They were presented with a list of forty-two items—ways of coping with tension—and instructed to check whether they did these "almost always," "often," "once in a while," or "never." One of the items on the list was eat constantly.

We found that 5 percent of the students checked that they ate constantly "almost always," 12 percent "often," 45 percent "once in a while," and 38 percent "never." So a majority of the people reported that at times they did indeed eat constantly as a response to feeling tense.[12]

John, a nineteen-year-old sophomore, was one of the students who reported that he almost always ate constantly when feeling tense. John found life at the university very stressful. He said that he had a fear of failure and talked about the pressures of meeting expectations of his family and friends as well as his own self-imposed pressures to excel. He said that he did not like being away from home for the long time period of the school semester. He had trouble falling asleep at night and often reported headaches and feelings of weakness. He reported that he very often felt tense. The things that brought on this tension were family problems, poor grades in a class, and weight gain. He reported that when he was tense, the things he did most often to relieve the feelings were to daydream or fantasize, listen to music, get some extra sleep, watch television, and eat constantly. John reported that he was overweight.

One may notice in John's case that some of the coping techniques he used to reduce stress had an escapist flavor (for example, daydreaming, watching television). Some psychologists have proposed that binging may have a similar effect, reducing unpleasant levels of self-awareness. If a person feels poorly about himself, binging may help him escape from these feelings. In this view, binging could have an effect similar to that of substance abuse. Heavy drinkers, for example, sometimes use alcohol to blot out awareness.

Todd Heatherton and Roy Baumeister, psychologists who have contributed to the development of this "escape" view of binge eating, noted that the perception of what one is doing during binge eating may become blurred. The ability to pay attention and exercise critical judgment may be diminished. Some bulimics report that they feel "unreal" during the experience. Others have reported that they begin binging with the expectation of blotting out negative feelings like depression. Inhibitions may vanish.[13] If this theory is correct, it could help explain the excesses that take place during binge eating.

6

Treatment of Eating Disorders

It is important for anyone with an eating disorder to seek help. For people with anorexia nervosa, the word *important* may not be strong enough. Words like *essential* and even *urgent* are not too strong. Anorexia is often fatal. About one in ten anorexics die from complications of the disorder. The longer the disorder is allowed to progress untreated, the greater the chance of a tragic outcome. The National Institute of Mental Health stresses the need for early treatment of all eating disorders, stating, "In any case, it cannot be overemphasized how important treatment is—the sooner, the better. The longer abnormal eating behaviors persist, the more difficult it is to overcome the disorder and its effects on the body."[1]

Getting People into Treatment

One of the difficulties that may be encountered in getting people who are afflicted with eating disorders into treatment is their resistance to seeking help. The patient's denial that there really is a problem is often part of the clinical picture in anorexia nervosa. The binging and purging of bulimia is often done in secret, making it difficult for others to know what is going on. Persuasion by others to seek help may be needed to get people into treatment.

In the case of anorexia, where the afflicted individual is often a teenager, her parents play an essential role in getting her into treatment. In some instances, the parents may not recognize the seriousness of the problem and this may cause delay in beginning treatment. Some parents may try to deal with the disorder themselves, which can prove very frustrating. The families of these patients are often emotionally and physically exhausted from trying to manage their children's behaviors.[2] Some have stayed up long nights with them or have attempted to physically stop their excessive exercising. Family members can become both frightened and angry.

The family physician can play a crucial role in diagnosing the problem and referring the patient to appropriate treatment. Because it is important that physicians be sensitive to the possible problem of eating disorders when talking with their adolescent and young adult patients, we might wonder, "Are physicians likely to ask questions about eating disorders when seeing such patients?" Researchers asked residents (physicians) in pediatric medicine what questions they would ask adolescent patients during office visits. The researchers found that questions about nutrition and eating disorders were not very high on the physicians' list. The physicians were more likely to ask about eating disorders if the patient was a female. The residents who had received more training in adolescent medicine during medical school were more likely to ask about nutritional issues.[3]

Common Symptoms of Eating Disorders

Symptoms	Anorexia Nervosa*	Bulimia Nervosa*	Binge Eating Disorder
Excessive weight loss in relatively short period of time	X		
Continuation of dieting although bone-thin	X		
Dissatisfaction with appearance; belief that body is fat, even though severely underweight	X	X	
Loss of monthly menstrual periods	X		
Unusual interest in food and development of strange eating rituals	X	X	
Eating in secret	X	X	X
Obsession with exercise	X		
Serious depression	X	X	X
Binging–consumption of large amounts of food		X	X
Vomiting or use of drugs to stimulate vomiting, bowel movements, and urination		X	
Binging but no noticeable weight gain		X	
Disappearance into bathroom for long periods of time to induce vomiting		X	
Abuse of drugs or alcohol		X	X

*Some individuals suffer from anorexia and bulimia and have symptoms of both disorders.
(Courtesy of the National Institutes of Health)

A comparison of anorexia, bulimia, and binge eating shows the common symptoms for each disorder.

Treatment of Anorexia Nervosa

A central task in the treatment of anorexia is to restore the patient to a normal weight level. In the early stages of anorexia, the patient may be treated in the physician's and therapist's offices. If the patient's weight has fallen far below acceptable levels, however, a program of building up weight would probably begin in a hospital. Feeding with tubes may be needed in cases where the medical situation is life-threatening. There is a hazard in rapid refeeding because this can cause the weakened cardiac system to collapse.[4] In the hospital, food intake can be carefully monitored—small amounts to begin with, gradually increased over time. When the patient's condition has improved, he or she can receive treatment outside the hospital.

Antidepressant and antianxiety medications have been tried with anorexic patients. At the present time, the value of these drugs for treating anorexia is unclear. Various kinds of psychotherapy have also been tried with anorexic patients. Sometimes the patient is given individual therapy. Sometimes

Help for Anorexic Patients

It should be stressed that many anorexic patients can be helped! Anorexic women were followed up eight years after the onset of the disorder. All had received treatment. Fifty-nine percent had a good recovery and were free of eating disorders.[5]

the whole family is involved, meeting in the therapist's office as a group. There is evidence that family therapy may be especially useful for younger anorexic patients.[6]

Treatment of Bulimia Nervosa

The American Psychiatric Association noted that if bulimia is not complicated by other demanding medical problems, hospitalization is rarely necessary.[7] Some of the situations that might require hospitalization are times when a medical emergency arises, when the bulimic patient becomes suicidal, or when the patient suffers from additional problems such as severe alcoholism or drug abuse.

The fact that many people with bulimia are depressed offers an obvious entry point for intervention: The strategy would be to treat the depression and see if the bulimic behaviors subside. The most convenient way to do this is to try an antidepressant drug. A variety of effective antidepressant drugs is available. When these drugs have been given to people with bulimia, the results have been good. About half of the patients treated with these drugs will abstain from bulimic behavior.[8]

Although antidepressant medications are very effective for many people with bulimia, not everyone is helped by them. Moreover, the drugs can have side effects such as making people sleepy or dizzy. Many people are uncomfortable taking the drugs. The question arises, Is there an alternative nondrug treatment for bulimia nervosa? The answer is yes. It is a form of psychotherapy called cognitive-behavioral therapy, and it appears to be as effective as antidepressant medications.

Cognitive-Behavioral Therapy

W. Stewart Agras and his colleagues at Stanford University describe a cognitive-behavioral approach to bulimia:[9]

(1) The patient monitors his or her own food intake, binge eating, and purging. The patient notes and records the circumstances that lead to binging.

(2) One of the goals of therapy is to work toward more normal eating patterns—at least three meals a day with more of the food eaten early in the day. A "behavior-change prescription" may be given to the patient to reshape his or her eating patterns.

(3) Education is provided about bulimia.

(4) In the dialog of therapy an attempt is made to change the patient's distorted ideas about food and eating. An effort is also made to change the patient's body image distortions.

(5) Relapse prevention procedures are taught. The patient learns strategies to deal with high-risk situations such as preparing food.

A study evaluating cognitive-behavioral therapy for bulimia followed up patients six months after completing a treatment program. Fifty-nine percent of the patients were no longer binging and purging.[10]

Suggestions for Bulimics

Let's put some details into this outline. How can a bulimic patient move toward the goal of normal eating? Craig Johnson and his colleagues of the Eating Disorders program at Northwestern University offered their bulimic patients a number of useful suggestions.[11] The first suggestion is more of a strong plea: Don't skip breakfast! Don't make yourself hungry.

A second suggestion has to do with those moments when a bulimic returns from school, work, or social activities. The patients are told to avoid the kitchen. "Many patients enter their homes and reflexively stop in the kitchen, where they quickly grab food."[12] These therapists advise patients to establish an alternative pattern when they enter the house, such as sorting the mail or reading the newspaper.

A trip to the kitchen presents a danger for people who binge. Advice to bingers is to avoid the kitchen upon returning home from school or work.

Third, if the patient does the cooking, she or he should minimize food handling and refrain from sampling the food as it cooks. This can be a dangerous time because bulimics often nibble at the food while preparing it.

Patients are also advised to sit at one designated place when they eat and to eat nowhere else. The television set should be turned off so that the patients maintain awareness of what they are eating. After eating, it is a good idea to become involved in some specific activity because the postmeal time is a high-risk time for feeling anxious and an impulse to purge.

Changing Beliefs

An important part of cognitive-behavioral therapy is changing the beliefs that promote eating disorders. Some of these beliefs have to do with eating and food; others have to do with the perception and evaluations of one's body. Here are three examples of beliefs that therapists might try to change:

(1) The patient may believe that the best way to prevent binging is to avoid food. However, avoiding regular meals is likely to be self-defeating. When hungry, the patient is likely to become preoccupied with food and may end up binging. In therapy, an effort should be made to change the patient's mind-set so that eating regular meals will be viewed as desirable.

(2) Bulimic patients often have incorrect ideas about what types of food are desirable to eat for controlling weight. Many bulimics believe that carbohydrates should be avoided.[13] In fact,

76

complex carbohydrates such as vegetables are good sources of nutrition in a weight-control program. Sound nutritional information should be presented as part of therapy to counteract the patient's current erroneous beliefs.

(3) Many patients with bulimia nervosa, as well as those with anorexia nervosa, have an exaggerated notion of the importance of being thin. Women who believe that they have to be unreasonably thin to be attractive are setting themselves a nearly impossible task that lays the groundwork for developing eating disorders. The therapist has the difficult job of persuading these patients that they can be attractive without looking like a fashion model.

Response Prevention Techniques

One approach that has been tried in treating bulimia is to teach patients ways of controlling their urges to binge and vomit. Here is a case report of how this has been done.[14] A twenty-one-year-old university student had been bulimic since the age of fifteen. She had episodes of bulimia almost every day since that time. When she came into the clinic for treatment, she was binging or overeating at least once a day and vomiting several times a day. She binged on such foods as cookies, crackers, pizza, bagels, and french fries. Afterward she felt bloated and anxious. She said she experienced a feeling of terror about gaining weight. She was able to diminish her anxiety by vomiting.

In treating the woman, the therapist used a behavioral therapy technique called "response prevention." With the therapist present, the patient ate either a large meal or lots of junk food. The therapist instructed her to pay attention to the anxiety-provoking thoughts that usually accompanied such binging and led her to vomit. This time he told her she was to focus on her discomfort but not vomit. She was to do this until her urge to vomit disappeared. It took over an hour, but she was able to do this.

The sessions were repeated over a period of forty-four days. As this therapy progressed, the patient's anxiety and urge to vomit began to decrease until they pretty well disappeared. During the ten months following response-prevention treatment, she reported only one episode of vomiting. Interestingly, binging also stopped, although it was not the direct target of the treatment. For this patient, response-prevention therapy was very effective. Long-term follow-up over several years would be needed to further evaluate the treatment.

Treatment of Binge Eating Disorder

Binge eating disorder has much in common with bulimia nervosa, so one might expect that the treatments would be similar. Indeed, stopping binging behavior is an important focus of treatment in both disorders. There is an important difference between the two disorders, however. Patients with binge eating disorder do not purge and so are likely to gain weight. Many become obese. Encouraging regular meals to reduce binging can be an effective treatment strategy for bulimics, but for obese binge eaters, there is an important qualification: The patient's meals should be carefully planned to promote healthy eating habits and weight loss. The goal for obese binge eaters is not only to stop binging, but to lose their unhealthy excess weight. Some researchers believe that binging should be controlled before dietary changes are made. If the patient is put on too restrictive a diet, there is the risk of increased binging. The problem requires careful management.

Programs using principles of behavior modification have been developed to help obese people lose weight. Here are some of the elements of such weight-reduction programs:[15]

(1) The goal for the patient is to expend more calories in daily activities than he or she eats. This should result in weight loss.

(2) Food intake is strictly monitored by the patient, using a food log or food diary. The log could be a simple piece of blank paper with instructions to write down everything eaten. Exercise should be recorded as well.

(3) Nutrition information is provided. Foods high in fat are avoided.

(4) A program of gradually increasing exercise is designed.

(5) The patient is asked to pay close attention to circumstances that tend to promote overeating and to take steps to control them. For example, if the patient tends to binge on sweets and salty snack foods, he or she is asked to remove them from the

home and not buy them when shopping. The suggestions for bulimics mentioned earlier, such as not rushing to the kitchen when returning home and not sampling food when cooking, make good sense for binge eaters as well.

(6) Regular weight checks are required.

(7) The patient should reward himself or herself after experiencing success in reducing weight. This could be patting oneself on the back, a trip to the movies, or whatever is pleasing—except for eating that high-calorie meal.

Traditional Psychotherapy

In our discussion of eating disorders, we have emphasized the use of antidepressant medications and cognitive-behavioral therapy. We have stressed these approaches to treatment because, in the case of bulimia at least, there is good evidence that they are effective. One might inquire whether more traditional types of psychotherapy—where the patient and therapist go more deeply into the patient's personal problems—can be helpful for people with eating disorders. In addressing this question, it is useful to recall that many people with eating disorders have significant emotional problems. Many people with anorexia and bulimia have experienced difficulties in their families, and have low self-esteem and perfectionistic tendencies. They are under stress, and many are depressed. Such psychological problems may be contributing causes to eating disorders and, if left unattended, may make them worse. When personal problems are bound up with the eating disorders, traditional psychotherapy should be considered to explore these issues.

Finding a Treatment Program

How does one seek treatment for an eating disorder? Consulting the family physician is usually a very good starting place, or you may want the help of a professional who is specially trained in eating disorders. If so, find out whether there are any eating disorder clinics in your community. University medical schools, as well as hospitals, may have such clinics. Organizations in the United States that may be able to provide information about such programs in your community are listed in the "For More Information" section at the back of the book.

People who are trying to cope with eating disorders often find it helpful to join support groups of people who have these problems. Dealing with an eating disorder can be a difficult process, and having the chance to talk with others who understand what you are going through can be quite helpful. As an example, Susan Owen and Mary Fullerton founded an eating disorder discussion group that met regularly at the University of Michigan.[16] The patients taking part in the group considered it a place where they felt secure enough to discuss their thoughts and feelings without fear of disapproval. The members felt less alone and saw the group as a place where they could give and receive support.

7

Society and Eating Disorders

I t has been said "beauty is in the eye of the beholder." What people consider beautiful may differ from person to person. Beauty is also defined by our culture. What we in the United States have come to accept as beautiful is not necessarily the same thing that someone native to the rain forests of the Amazon or the Rift Valley of Africa might consider beautiful. Men of the Turkana people who live in East Africa adorn themselves by wearing plugs in their lips and a pack of clay on top of their head capped with an ostrich feather. The culture in which they live tells them that this is the thing to do, that it is attractive, desirable, even proper. American women, on the other hand, have been raised to pierce their ears to wear earrings and to use lipstick to look attractive. Many people also sport body tattoos and piercings.

What we learn to accept as beautiful about the human

body is largely determined by the cultural messages we receive. And what does our own culture tell us about a beautiful body—particularly for a woman? Perhaps we can answer this by asking, Who are the role models for beauty and what do they look like? Beauty contest participants, movie stars, television stars, and high-fashion models are good places to start.

Consider fashion models. What do the staffs of model agencies look for in terms of physical characteristics for girls who want to become fashion models? I was curious, so I called a modeling agency and was told, "five-nine and a proportionate body build." That sounds statuesque. Try looking through the pages of upscale women's magazines and count how many of the women have a body build on the heavy side. Then try it for an average build, and finally for a thin build. What do you find? In her book *Beauty Bound,* Rita Freedman cited an advertisement from a department store that used such phrases as "bean lean," "narrow as an arrow," "pencil thin," and "slender as the night" to convey its message of feminine form.[1] Researchers have studied Miss America winners and found that over the years they have become thinner.[2]

If society's message is that to be thin is to be beautiful, where does that leave overweight people? In Shakespeare's play *Julius Caesar,* Caesar remarked, "Let me have men about me that are fat." He distrusted men with "a lean and hungry look."[3] Quite the opposite is the case today. Society does not

Fashion models are typically very thin, sending a message to young people that thin is beautiful.

treat overweight people kindly. They are often the butt of jokes and experience discrimination.

Changing Concepts of Beauty

Remember the equation that seems to be part of the thought processes of many young women with eating disorders, thinness = beauty = popularity? What would happen if we changed the first part of the equation and said instead, "plumpness = beauty = popularity"? Such thinking might put a damper on fasting behavior. Are you shaking your head and saying it could not happen, that nobody would ever equate plumpness with beauty? In the 1880s, a British visitor to the United States was surprised by the numbers of buxom, matronly women he saw. Another visitor was impressed by American women's fear of becoming too thin. He wrote that they were constantly weighing themselves, and every ounce of increase in weight brought on delight. One woman he met boasted of gaining eighteen pounds. A writer of the period wrote that plumpness is beautiful.[4]

Cultural ideas of what is beautiful are not etched in stone. Before the advent of these more full-figured women of the 1880s, the desired figure for a woman was described as willowy. The ideal woman was thought of as pale and frail . . . someone who might break in half if exposed to a stiff breeze.[5]

So cultural views about what is a desirable body shape change from time to time. In some eras women have been told they should be thin, other times plump. The question that arises is, Does it make any more sense for a modern woman to lose eighteen pounds to be very thin than for her 1880 counterpart to gain eighteen pounds to be pleasingly plump? The problem arises when people take to heart the ideas that are currently in vogue to the point that they feel miserable that they do not look the way they think they should. If they act on these feelings by severely restricting food intake, they open themselves up to the risk of developing eating disorders.

Gender Differences in Body Images

Imagine you are presented with a series of drawings showing a man. In the first drawing, the man is rather thin. In each succeeding picture the man is somewhat heavier. By the last picture, the man is clearly overweight. The drawings are placed on a rulerlike scale. If you are a male student, you are asked to pick a spot on the scale that represents (1) your current appearance, (2) what you want to look like, and (3) what you feel is most attractive to the opposite sex.

Now this procedure is similar to the study we described in Chapter 4 for female patients with bulimia nervosa. But this time we are using a sample of normal young men. When the study was carried out on college men, the results showed that the average ratings of actual body size, desired body size, and the body that would please the opposite sex were close together. There were no real differences between the three ratings.[6] As a group, these young men saw no need to have thinner bodies.

When the same experiment was carried out with normal young women, this time using drawings of women, the results were quite different. The women would have liked their bodies to be considerably thinner than they were and believed that this thinner body is what men would find attractive.[7] It is important to stress that the subjects were normal young women without eating disorders. As we saw in Chapter 4, when the women studied had eating disorders, the difference between their perceptions of their bodies and what they wanted to look like was even more pronounced. What this study shows is that many normal young women have accepted

When men and women were both asked about their actual body sizes, the men saw no need to be thinner while the women would have liked to be thinner.

the ideas that (1) women should be thin, (2) men like thin women, and (3) they themselves are too heavy. Interestingly, when men were asked to look at the same drawings of women and pick out the figure they found most attractive, they tended to pick one that is closer to what women say they currently look like than the thinner figure women think they should have.[8]

If men are not unhappy with the way women look and women are driving themselves to be thinner, what in the world is going on? Research suggests that the importance of a thin body seeps into the awareness of girls at an early age. A study found that body build was associated with girls' feeling of self-esteem as early as the fourth grade. Thinner girls felt more popular and attractive.[9] Consciousness about weight occurs long before adolescence in many girls, and by adolescence, dieting to control weight is common. Recent surveys have shown that nearly half of adolescent girls are trying to lose weight.[10] In a study reported in 1992, 70 percent of the American girls studied wanted to be thinner than their current size.[11] The message of thinness has been absorbed by many, if not most, of the adolescent girls in our society.

Culture and Body Image

Why are girls more likely than boys to develop this heightened concern about weight? The answer probably lies in the fact that in our culture—and indeed in many other cultures as well—a stronger emphasis is placed on beauty in women than in men. Beauty is thought to be more important in women. In studies in which people are asked about the characteristics they would look for in a date or a mate, men are more likely to mention physical attractiveness when considering a woman than women are when considering a man.[12] It may not seem fair, but today's young women grow up in such a culture and it can make a difference in their attitudes and behavior, including their decision to diet.

There are probably a variety of reasons why more emphasis has been given to physical attractiveness in women than in men. One line of explanation for this difference involves the different roles society has traditionally given to men and women. It was not that many years ago that career options were very limited for women. The vocation expected for most women was to be a wife, homemaker, and mother. Being physically attractive was a considerable advantage for women in making a good marriage. In contrast, the likelihood of being a good provider was often judged the important thing for a prospective husband.

Society cultivated these different gender roles in the way children were raised. Boys were raised to develop independence, girls to be more focused on relationships and homemaking skills. Girls learned that they were supposed to be neat and pretty. When they were, they were complimented and accepted.[13] A study revealed that the girls in children's books were often concerned about how they looked, whereas the boys never were.[14]

Western civilization and American culture in particular have been changing rapidly. The pace of change sometimes seems dizzying. Recent studies suggest that there are now few differences in the way boys and girls are being raised.[15] In many homes the rigid gender roles of yesteryear have been swept away. Examples of independent, successful women are everywhere. The explanation for the large gender differences in eating disorders based on traditional sex roles no longer fits well. Yet if anything, the number of cases of anorexia nervosa is rising! This is a puzzle.

The concept of cultural lag may be helpful here. Changes in some aspects of a culture may occur while other aspects remain fixed in place. The pressure for women to marry is less strong than in earlier generations, but the need felt by women to be attractive remains very strong. With major changes taking place in our society, it will be interesting to see whether this gender difference decreases over the years.

Even while stressing the importance of our culture's messages in the development of eating disorders, it should be noted that some cases of anorexia have been found in non-Western societies where being thin is not seen as the virtue it is here. In Bangalore, India, anorexic children were found in traditional families in which the children had never even left the village; they had no exposure to Western ideas about thinness. In Hong Kong, researchers studying anorexics found that the pressure to become thin for the sake of beauty was not typical. These young anorexic people reported a variety of other stress-producing situations in their lives such as examination pressures, relationship difficulties, and conflicts with parents. Most of the anorexics in the Hong Kong studies indicated that the avoidance of being fat did not play a role in their disorders.[16] So while a social message that thin is beautiful provides a clear basis for anorexia in Western societies like the United States, it may not be a necessary condition for the development of the disorder. It can occur in other circumstances, which brings us back full circle to our earlier accounts of women who fasted for reasons of piety.

8

Prevention of Eating Disorders

We do not know a great deal about the best ways to prevent eating disorders. Compared with a problem like drug abuse where many different programs have been developed and evaluated, work on the prevention of eating disorders is still in its early stages. Prevention programs are possible on several levels: school, family, and community.

Researcher Catherine Shisslak and her colleagues recommended that educational programs in the schools should begin in junior high school.[1] The goal would be to increase students' understanding and appreciation of their bodies and their individual needs. Here is one of their examples of a classroom exercise dealing with nutrition:

> *Materials.* A chart containing daily caloric requirements for girls of different heights and weights, a list of the caloric

contents of a variety of common foods, and a list of the calories consumed during common exercises will be needed.

Assignments. Devise a day's menu and activity schedule for each of the following conditions: (a) your weight is fine and you want to maintain it; (b) you are underweight and want to gain 1 lb a week (500 extra calories a day); (c) you want to lose 1 lb a week (500 fewer calories a day).

Class discussion. In class, the teacher can raise the following questions for student consideration.

1. How satisfying does each menu look?

2. To lose weight, did you reduce calories, increase exercise, or both?

3. Why is it important to reduce weight gradually rather than all at once? (You function better emotionally, you keep more weight off, you lose fat rather than muscle and water, and you don't disrupt your menstrual cycle.)[2]

At the senior high school level, information can be introduced on the health consequences of anorexia and bulimia. Students could be exposed to guest speakers, particularly healthy, successful women who practice good nutrition in their daily lives.

While teaching about eating disorders in the schools as part of health education makes good sense, it has to be done with care. As with suicide education, eating disorders should not be glamorized or overemphasized. While pointing out the risks of eating disorders, the emphasis should be placed on a positive lifestyle and sensible, healthy nutrition.

Prevention in the Family

Children develop many of their own behavior patterns by observing and then modeling what their parents do. If parents practice good nutrition in their choice of foods, the children are likely to accept that behavior as a standard. If parents practice poor nutrition or have eating disorders of their own, the children may model these behaviors. Parent education about nutrition and the warning signs of eating disorders is needed. Parent-Teacher Associations could get involved in setting up programs.

Destructive patterns of parent-child relationships are probably involved in many cases of eating disorders. Even before eating disorders are clear-cut and diagnosable, there is often evidence of poor parent-child communication in the family as well as lack of cohesion in the way the family functions.[3] Such patterns of family interaction are not new to researchers and therapists; much the same can be said about many families in which there is adolescent drug abuse, truancy, runaway behavior, and suicide. Improving family interactions to make them more positive, constructive, and supportive is an important goal, but the effort is too often made only after a serious problem such as an eating disorder has surfaced. At this point, professional help is often needed to deal with the problem.

Prevention in the Community

An important strategy for prevention of eating disorders in the community is additional education about these disorders for adults who have significant contact with young people. This would include teachers, counselors, coaches, doctors, nurses, and therapists. When such people know more about eating disorders, they are better able to identify at-risk young people and direct them toward getting the help they need. They can help make the goal of early treatment a reality.

Personal Prevention

At some point, prevention of eating disorders comes down to individual choices and decisions. Responsibility will eventually fall on each individual—to choose what to eat, how much to eat, and how much to exercise. In making these choices, here are some thoughts to consider:

Body Image. What kind of body image do you now have of yourself? Are you reasonably satisfied, or are you dissatisfied? If you are dissatisfied, what do you think you should look like? Now think about this "should-look-like" image. Is this your own idea, or could it come from somewhere else? Are you trying to please yourself, or to look a certain way for others? Does your ideal body image come from fashion ads or from television? Think about it, then ask yourself what is really right for you.

Height–Weight Charts. In thinking about weight, take a look at the height–weight charts on pages 97 and 98. They are not etched in stone, but are useful targets for maintaining good health. If you fall inside the target range, fine! If you fall only slightly outside the target range, it is probably not worth worrying about. But if you are way outside the range, it would make sense to consult your doctor and see what you can do to improve the situation.

A Healthy Diet. Eating regular meals, including breakfast, may help prevent weight problems. It is a mistake to starve yourself. You will probably just get hungry and end up eating too much. The choice of foods is important. Good selection will help maintain a desirable weight and help prevent such diseases as heart disease and cancer. The U.S. Department of Agriculture along with the Department of Health and Human Services has published a helpful booklet entitled "Nutrition and Your Health: Dietary Guidelines for Americans."[4] If you would like to look through the booklet, ask your school librarian to request a copy from the Department of Agriculture.

How well are American teenagers doing now in following such guidelines for maintaining reasonable weights? Are they trying to keep weight at desirable levels by good food selection and exercise, or are they falling into questionable practices such as missing meals and taking diet pills? Results from surveys suggest that teenage girls are doing both. In one study, 32 percent of the girls surveyed said they were increasing exercise, 27 percent said they were eating more fruits and vegetables, 24 percent said they were eliminating sweets and junk food, and 26 percent said they were cutting back on

TABLE OF DESIRABLE WEIGHTS FOR WOMEN[5]

Height	Average Weight	Acceptable Weight Range
4'10"	102	92–119
4'11"	104	94–122
5' 0"	107	96–125
5' 1"	110	99–128
5' 2"	113	102–131
5' 3"	116	105–134
5' 4"	120	108–138
5' 5"	123	111–142
5' 6"	128	114–146
5' 7"	132	118–150
5' 8"	136	122–154
5' 9"	140	126–158
5'10"	144	130–163
5'11"	148	134–168

The figures are for height without shoes, weight without clothes. The average weight for young teenage girls is slightly lower than the figures posted above.

TABLE OF DESIRABLE WEIGHTS FOR MEN[6]

Height	Average Weight	Acceptable Weight Range
5' 2"	123	112–141
5' 3"	127	115–144
5' 4"	130	118–148
5' 5"	133	121–152
5' 6"	136	124–156
5' 7"	140	128–161
5' 8"	145	132–166
5' 9"	149	136–170
5'10"	153	140–174
5'11"	158	144–179
6' 0"	166	148–184
6' 1"	166	152–189
6' 2"	171	156–194
6' 3"	176	160–199
6' 4"	181	164–204

The figures are for height without shoes, weight without clothes. The average weight for young teenage boys is slightly lower than the figures posted above.

foods high in fat content.[7] Results from another survey, however, indicated that 33 percent of the girls were fasting at times, 45 percent skipped meals, and 11 percent used diet pills.[8] Such habits can lay the groundwork for the development of eating disorders.

Emotional Health. Eating disorders often have an emotional basis. Keeping a good mental health balance will help prevent eating disorders as well as many other problems. Depression, in particular, has been linked to eating disorders. If you often feel depressed, consider professional help.

Future Research

One of the keys to prevention of eating disorders is better understanding of the problem. While much has been learned about eating disorders, it is clear that much remains to be learned. Research is being carried out on eating disorders in the United States and in other countries.

The Woman's Health Research Institute and the Osteoporosis Center at Women's Hospital in Baton Rouge, Louisiana, have designed a study to see whether weight training and calcium supplements in combination with psychotherapy and reeducation can increase the bone mass of anorexic women.[9] In Minnesota, researchers are following seventh- to tenth-grade students over a period of years, looking at the relation of family functioning, school behaviors, and academic performance and the development of eating disorders. The researchers are obtaining information from the

Food Guide Pyramid
A Guide to Daily Food Choices

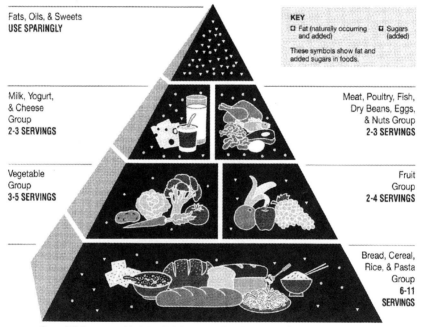

Fats, Oils, & Sweets
USE SPARINGLY

KEY
□ Fat (naturally occurring and added)   ■ Sugars (added)
These symbols show fat and added sugars in foods.

Milk, Yogurt, & Cheese Group
2-3 SERVINGS

Meat, Poultry, Fish, Dry Beans, Eggs, & Nuts Group
2-3 SERVINGS

Vegetable Group
3-5 SERVINGS

Fruit Group
2-4 SERVINGS

Bread, Cereal, Rice, & Pasta Group
6-11 SERVINGS

Source: U.S. Department of Agriculture/U.S. Department of Health and Human Services

The food guide pyramid shows that a healthy diet includes many grains, fruits, and vegetables and limited foods high in fats and oils.

students each year to study the development of possible problems.[10]

These are just two of many studies that are looking at different aspects of eating disorders, ranging from the biological to the social. With increased knowledge about eating disorders, we can look forward to more effective approaches to treatment and prevention.

Q & A

Q: Do eating disorders happen mainly to women?

A: The eating disorders of anorexia and bulimia afflict women much more often than men. Binge eating disorder affects men and women about equally.

Q: Why are women particularly vulnerable to anorexia and bulimia?

A: Physical attractiveness is considered in most societies to be more important for women than for men. Many women are concerned about becoming heavy and may take extreme measures to avoid gaining weight.

Q: Which of the eating disorders is most dangerous?

A: They all can be serious problems, but anorexia is especially worrisome because many young people die from complications of the disorder.

Q: Is early treatment important for anorexia?

A: Very. The longer anorexia is left untreated, the more serious it is likely to become.

Q: Is it easy to tell if a friend is bulimic?

A: Not unless she tells you. The purging behaviors of the bulimic are usually carried out in private.

Q: Are there effective treatments for bulimia?

A: Both antidepressive medicines and cognitive-behavioral therapy are effective treatments for many bulimic patients.

Q: How is binge eating disorder different from bulimia?

A: Bulimics binge and then purge to prevent weight gain. People with binge eating disorder simply binge; as a result, many become obese.

Q: What are the consequences of binge eating disorder?

A: Binge eaters who become obese have increased risks of serious diseases such as heart disease. Obese people have higher death rates than people of normal weight.

Q: What are some ways of preventing eating disorders?

A: Eating regular, well-balanced meals is desirable. It is also important not to buy into the idea that one has to be very thin to be attractive. This idea underlies much of the anorexia and bulimia we see today.

Q: How can I get help for an eating disorder?

A: First, consult with your family doctor. Then, check local hospitals and universities to see if there are any eating disorder clinics in your area.

Eating Disorders Timeline

1300s—Anorexia is reported as a way of achieving piety.

1743—English medical dictionary described "true boulimus," similar to modern-day eating disorders.

1700 —Reports of fasting girls—women who supposedly ate
–1900 little or nothing and survived.

1873—Anorexia nervosa was described by Charles Lasègue in France. At about the same time, William Gull in England made contributions to the understanding of the disorder.

1959—Publication of Albert Stunkard's paper led to the identification of binge eating disorder.

1970s—Bulimia nervosa was identified as an eating disorder by researchers studying anorexia.

1981—*Newsweek* magazine called this year "The Year of the Binge-Purge Syndrome."

1994—Binge eating disorder was included in the appendix of the *Diagnostic and Statistical Manual of Mental Disorders* of the American Psychiatric Association.

For More Information

American Anorexia/Bulimia Association, Inc. (AABA)
165 West 46th Street, Suite 1108
New York, NY 10036
212-575-6200
E-mail: amanbu@aol.com
Website: <www.aabainc.org>

Anorexia Nervosa & Related
Eating Disorders (ANRED)
P.O. Box 5102
Eugene, OR 97405
541-344-1144
Website: <www.anred.com>

Bulimia Anorexia Self Help, Inc. (BASH)
6125 Clayton Avenue, Suite 215
St. Louis, MO 63139
314-567-4080

Center for the Study of Anorexia and Bulimia
1841 Broadway, Fourth Floor
New York, NY 10023
212-333-3444

National Anorex Aid Society (NAAS)
Harding Hospital
1925 East Dublin Granville Road
Columbus, OH 43229
614-436-1112

**National Association of Anorexia Nervosa and
Associated Disorders (ANAD)**
P.O. Box 7
Highland Park, IL 60035
847-831-3438
E-mail: anad20@aol.com
Website: <members.aol.com/anad20/index.html>

National Eating Disorders Organization
6655 South Yale Avenue
Tulsa, OK 74136
918-481-4044
Website: <www.laureate.com>

Overeaters Anonymous
P.O. Box 92870
Los Angeles, CA 90009
310-618-8835
Website: <http://recovery.hiwaay.net>

Chapter Notes

Chapter 1. Introduction

1. H. Bruch, *The Golden Cage: The Enigma of Anorexia Nervosa* (Cambridge, Mass.: Harvard University Press, 1978), pp. 1–3.

2. "Eating Disorders" (Rockville, Md.: National Institute of Mental Health, 1993), pp. 3–4.

3. A. Stunkard, "A Description of Eating Disorders in 1932," *American Journal of Psychiatry*, vol. 147, March 1990, p. 266.

4. C. Jakobovits, P. Halstead, L. Kelley, D.A. Roe, and C.M. Young, "Eating Habits and Nutrient Intakes of College Women over a Thirty Year Period," *Journal of the American Dietetic Association*, vol. 71, October 1977.

5. J. Polivy and C.P. Herman, "Diagnosis and Treatment of Normal Eating," *Journal of Consulting and Clinical Psychology*, vol. 55, October 1987, p. 636; J.C. Rosen and J. Gross, "Prevalence of Weight Reducing and Weight Gaining in Adolescent Girls and Boys," *Health Psychology*, vol. 6, 1987; S.A. French, C.L. Perry, G.R. Leon, and J.A. Fulkerson, "Dieting Behaviors and Weight Change History in Female Adolescents," *Health Psychology*, vol. 14, November 1995.

6. Polivy and Herman, p. 641.

7. R.H. Lowie, *Indians of the Plains* (Garden City, N.Y.: McGraw-Hill Book Co., Inc., 1954), p. 157.

8. P. Farb and G. Armelagos, *Consuming Passions: The Anthropology of Eating* (Boston: Houghton Mifflin, 1980), p. 7.

9. Ibid., p. 8.

Chapter 2. History of Eating Disorders

1. J.J. Brumberg, *Fasting Girls: The Emergence of Anorexia Nervosa as a Modern Disease* (Cambridge, Mass.: Harvard University Press, 1988), pp. 119, 129–134.

2. Ibid., pp. 115–116, 118–125.

3. W.W. Gull, "Anorexia Nervosa (Apepsia Hysterica, Anorexia Hysterica)," *Transactions of the Clinical Society of London*, vol. 7, 1874, pp. 22–23, cited in M. Strober, "Anorexia Nervosa: History and Psychological Concepts," in K.D. Brownell and J.P. Foreyt eds., *Handbook of Eating Disorders: Physiology, Psychology, and Treatment of Obesity, Anorexia, and Bulimia* (New York: Basic Books, 1986), p. 234.

4. Brumberg, pp. 41–46.

5. Ibid., pp. 41, 44–45.

6. Ibid., p. 47.

7. Ibid., pp. 55–60.

8. Ibid., p. 93.

9. T.C. Allbutt, "Neuroses of the Stomach and Other Parts of the Abdomen," in T.C. Allbutt and H.D. Rolleston, eds., *A System of Medicine*, vol. 3 (London: Macmillan, 1910), p. 398, cited in A.S. Kaplan and D.B. Woodside, "Biological Aspects of Anorexia Nervosa and Bulimia Nervosa," *Journal of Consulting and Clinical Psychology*, vol. 55, October 1987, p. 645.

10. W. Scott, "Personality Parade," *Parade*, September 15, 1996, p. 2.

11. M. Boskind-White and W.C. White, Jr., "Bulimarexia: A Historical-Sociocultural Perspective," in K.D. Brownell and J.P. Foreyt, eds., *Handbook of Eating Disorders: Physiology, Psychology, and Treatment of Obesity, Anorexia, and Bulimia* (New York: Basic Books, 1986), p. 354.

12. R. James, *A Medical Dictionary* (London: T. Osborne, 1743), cited in A. Stunkard, "A Description of Eating Disorders in 1932," *American Journal of Psychiatry*, vol. 147, March 1990, p. 264.

13. *Newsweek*, January 4, 1981, p. 26.

14. B. Schlesier-Stropp, "Bulimia: A Review of the Literature," *Psychological Bulletin*, vol. 95, March 1984, pp. 247–248.

15. A.J. Stunkard, "Eating Patterns and Obesity," *Psychiatric Quarterly*, vol. 33, Summer 1959.

16. P. Farb and G. Armelagos, *Consuming Passions: The Anthropology of Eating* (Boston: Houghton Mifflin, 1980), p. 196.

17. C.M. Shisslak, M. Crago, and L.S. Estes, "The Spectrum of Eating Disturbances," *International Journal of Eating Disorders*, vol. 18, November 1995, p. 210; R.L. Spitzer et al., "Binge Eating Disorder: Its Further Validation in a Multisite Study," *International Journal of Eating Disorders*, vol. 13, March 1993.

Chapter 3. What Is Anorexia Nervosa?

1. C.A. Kirschock, "Dying for a Candy Bar," in "The Skinnier I Got, the Fatter I Felt," *Mademoiselle*, March 1996, p. 164.

2. American Psychiatric Association, "Practice Guideline for Eating Disorders," *American Journal of Psychiatry*, vol. 150, February 1993.

3. R.M. Gardner and E.D. Bokenkamp, "The Role of Sensory and Nonsensory Factors in Body Size Estimations of Eating Disorder Subjects," *Journal of Clinical Psychology*, vol. 52, January 1996, p. 3.

4. American Psychiatric Association, "Practice Guideline for Eating Disorders."

5. K.J. Zerbe, "Anorexia Nervosa and Bulimia Nervosa: When the Pursuit of Bodily Perfection Becomes a Killer," *Postgraduate Medicine*, vol. 99, January 1996, p. 161.

6. P.S. Mehler, "Eating Disorders: 1. Anorexia Nervosa," *Hospital Practice*, vol. 31, January 15, 1996, pp. 110–111.

7. Ibid., p. 112.

8. A.A. Anderson, P.J. Woodward, and N. LaFrance, "Bone Mineral Density of Eating Disorder Subgroups," *International Journal of Eating Disorders*, vol. 18, December 1995.

9. A.S. Kaplan and D.B. Woodside, "Biological Aspects of Anorexia Nervosa and Bulimia Nervosa," *Journal of Consulting and Clinical Psychology*, vol. 55, October 1987, p. 646.

10. Ibid., pp. 645–646.

11. Mehler, p. 117.

12. "Eating Disorders" (Rockville, Md.: National Institute of Mental Health, 1993), p. 5.

13. K. Kingston, G. Szmukler, D. Andrewes, B. Tress, and P. Desmond, "Neuropsychological and Structural Brain Changes in Anorexia Nervosa Before and After Refeeding," *Psychological Medicine*, vol. 26, January 1996.

14. Mehler, p. 109.

15. M. Strober and L.L. Humphrey, "Familial Contributions to the Etiology and Course of Anorexia Nervosa and Bulimia," *Journal of Consulting and Clinical Psychology*, vol. 55, October 1987, p. 654.

16. Ibid.

17. Ibid.

18. P.E. Garfinkel, D.M. Garner, J. Rose, P.L. Darby, J.S. Brandos, J. O'Hanlon, and N. Walsh, "A Comparison of Characteristics in Families of Patients with Anorexia Nervosa and Normal Controls," *Psychological Medicine*, vol. 13, November 1983.

19. L.L. Humphrey, "Structural Analysis of Parent-Child Relationships in Eating Disorders," *Journal of Abnormal Psychology*, vol. 95, November 1986, p. 395.

20. A. Laws and J. M. Golding, "Sexual Assault History and Eating Disorder Symptoms Among White, Hispanic, and African-American Women and Men," *American Journal of Public Health*, vol. 86, April 1996.

21. Ibid., pp. 580–581; Zerbe, p. 164.

22. H. Bruch, *The Golden Cage: The Enigma of Anorexia Nervosa* (Cambridge, Mass.: Harvard University Press, 1978), pp. 109–112.

23. N. J. Kolodny, *When Food's a Foe: How to Confront and Conquer Eating Disorders* (Boston: Little, Brown, 1992), pp. 38–39.

24. Ibid., p. 110.

25. T. D. Brewerton, "Toward a Unified Theory of Serotonin Dysregulation in Eating and Related Disorders," *Psychoneuroendocrinology*, vol. 20, issue 6, 1995.

26. Strober and Humphrey, p. 656.

27. D. M. Garner, M. P. Olmstead, and J. Polivy, "Development and Validation of a Multidimensional Eating Disorder Inventory for Anorexia Nervosa and Bulimia," *International Journal of Eating Disorders*, vol. 2, 1983. See also Humphrey, p. 400.

28. "Eating Disorders," p. 2.

29. Bruch, p. 74.

30. M. P. Levine, *How Schools Can Help Combat Student Eating Disorders: Anorexia Nervosa and Bulimia* (Washington, D.C.: National Education Association, 1987), p. 46.

31. Bruch, pp. 81–82.

32. Humphrey, Table 1, p. 398.

33. M. A. Marrazzi, J. P. Bacon, J. Kinzie, and E. D. Luby, "Naltrexone Use in the Treatment of Anorexia Nervosa and Bulimia Nervosa," *International Clinical Psychopharmacology*, vol. 10, September 1995.

34. S.G. Boodman, "The Medical Costs of Being Young, Female and the Best," *The Washington Post*, July 30, 1996, Health section, p. 9; W. Plummer et al., "Dying for a Medal," *People Weekly*, August 22, 1994.

35. Boodman, p. 12.

36. "Gymnastics, Figure Skating Address Serious Issues," *CAAWS-ACTION*, Autumn 1995.

37. B. Azer, "Public Scrutiny Sparks Some Eating Disorders," *Monitor* (American Psychological Association), July 1996, p. 33.

38. K.L. Bennell, S.A. Malcolm, S.A. Thomas, P.R. Ebeling, P.R. McCrory, J.D. Wank, and P.D. Brukner, "Risk Factors for Stress Fractures in Female Track-and-Field Athletes: A Retrospective Analysis," *Clinical Journal of Sports Medicine*, vol. 5, October 1995.

Chapter 4. What Is Bulimia Nervosa?

1. K.A. Haynes, "Zina Garrison-Jackson: Tennis Star's Battle Against Bulimia," *Ebony*, June 1993.

2. H.W. Hoek, A.I.M. Bartelds, J.J.F. Bosveld, Y. van der Graaf, V.E.L. Limpens, M. Maiwald, and C.J.K. Spaaij, "Impact of Urbanization on Detection Rates of Eating Disorders," *American Journal of Psychiatry*, vol. 152, September 1995, p. 1275.

3. American Psychiatric Association, "Practice Guideline for Eating Disorders," *American Journal of Psychiatry*, vol. 150, February 1993, p. 212.

4. R. Davis, R.J. Freeman, and D.M. Garner, "A Naturalistic Investigation of Eating Behavior in Bulimia Nervosa," *Journal of Consulting and Clinical Psychology*, vol. 56, April 1988, p. 275.

5. Ibid., p. 276.

6. P.S. Mehler, "Eating Disorders: 2. Bulimia Nervosa," *Hospital Practice*, February 15, 1996, p. 114.

7. Ibid., pp. 114–115.

8. A. Stunkard, "A Description of Eating Disorders in 1932," *American Journal of Psychiatry*, vol. 147, March 1990, p. 266.

9. A.S. Kaplan and D.B. Woodside, "Biological Aspects of Anorexia Nervosa and Bulimia Nervosa," *Journal of Consulting and Clinical Psychology*, vol. 55, October 1987, p. 646.

10. Mehler, p. 108.

11. Ibid., pp. 110, 113.

12. Ibid., p. 123.

13. Ibid., p. 108.

14. L.R. Hazelton and M.P. Faine, "Diagnosis and Dental Management of Eating Disorder Patients," *International Journal of Prosthodontics*, vol. 9, January–February 1996.

15. Ibid., pp. 69–70.

16. M. Strober and L.L. Humphrey, "Familial Contributions to the Etiology and Course of Anorexia Nervosa and Bulimia," *Journal of Consulting and Clinical Psychology*, vol. 55, October 1987, p. 655.

17. L.L. Humphrey, "Structural Analysis of Parent-Child Relationships in Eating Disorders," *Journal of Abnormal Psychology*, vol. 95, November 1986.

18. P.E. Garfinkel, E. Lin, P. Goering, C. Spegg, D.S. Goldbloom, S. Kennedy, A.S. Kaplan, and D.B. Woodside, "Bulimia Nervosa in a Canadian Community Sample: Prevalence and Comparison of Subgroups," *American Journal of Psychiatry*, vol. 152, July 1995, pp. 1054–1055.

19. D.A. Williamson, M.L. Kelley, C.J. Davis, L. Ruggiero, and D.C. Blouin, "Psychopathology of Eating Disorders: A Controlled Comparison of Bulimic, Obese, and Normal Subjects," *Journal of Consulting and Clinical Psychology*, vol. 53, April 1985, p. 163.

20. S.R. Sunday, K.A. Halmi, and A. Einhorn, "The Yale-Brown-Cornell Eating Disorder Scale: A New Scale to Assess Eating Disorder Symptomology," *International Journal of Eating Disorders*, vol. 18, November 1995, p. 243.

21. Ibid., Table 3, p. 240.

22. J.C. Rosen and H. Leitenberg, "Bulimia Nervosa: Treatment with Exposure and Response Prevention," *Behavior Therapy*, vol. 13, January 1982.

23 T.F. Heatherton and R.F.Baumeister, "Binge Eating as Escape from Self-Awareness," *Psychological Bulletin*, vol. 110, July 1991, p. 92.

24. Ibid.

25. C.M. Shisslak, T. Perse, and M. Crago, "Co-existence of Bulimia Nervosa and Mania: A Literature Review and Case Report," *Comprehensive Psychiatry*, vol. 32, March–April 1991, p. 182.

26. Heatherton, p. 92.

27. M.A. Katzman and S.A. Wolchick, "Bulimia and Binge Eating in College Women: A Comparison of Personality and Behavioral Characteristics," *Journal of Consulting and Clinical Psychology*, vol. 52, June 1984, p. 423.

28. Shisslak, pp. 182–183.

29. D.B. Herzog, D.K. Norman, N.A. Regotti, and M. Pepose, "Frequency of Bulimic Behaviors and Associated Social Maladjustment in Female Graduate Students," *Journal of Psychiatric Research*, vol. 20, issue 4, 1986, pp. 359–360.

30. P.L. Hewitt, G.L. Flett, and E. Ediger, "Perfectionism Traits and Perfectionistic Self-Presentation in Eating Disorder Attitudes, Characteristics and Symptoms," *International Journal of Eating Disorders*, vol. 18, December 1995, p. 322.

31. P.M. Keel and J.E. Mitchell, "Outcome in Bulimia Nervosa," *American Journal of Psychiatry*, vol. 154, March 1997.

Chapter 5. What Is Binge Eating Disorder?

1. R.L. Spitzer et al., "Binge Eating Disorder: Its Further Validation in a Multisite Study," *International Journal of Eating Disorders*, vol. 13, April 1993.

2. J. Polivy and C.P. Herman, "Dieting and Binging: A Causal Analysis," *American Psychologist*, vol. 40, February 1985, p. 195. See also the original study, A. Keys, J. Brozek, A. Henschel, O. Mickelsen, and H.L. Taylor, *The Biology of Human Starvation* (Minneapolis: University of Minnesota Press, 1950).

3. For a brief listing of the proposed benchmarks for the diagnosis of binge eating disorder, see M.L. Brody, B.T. Walsh, and M.T. Devlin, "Binge Eating Disorder: Reliability and Validity of a New Diagnostic Category," *Journal of Consulting and Clinical Psychology*, vol. 62, April 1994, Table 1, p. 383.

4. G.A. Bray, "Effects of Obesity on Health and Happiness," in K.D. Brownell and J.P. Foreyt (eds.), *Handbook of Eating Disorders: Physiology, Psychology, and Treatment of Obesity, Anorexia, and Bulimia* (New York: Basic Books, 1986), p. 1.

5. Ibid.

6. J.P. Foreyt, "Issues in the Assessment and Treatment of Obesity," *Journal of Consulting and Clinical Psychology*, vol. 55, October 1987; The Merck Manual of Diagnosis and Therapy, vol. 1, 15th ed. (Rahway, N.J.: Merck & Co., 1987), p. 733.

7. S.Z. Yanovski, J.E. Nelson, B.K. Dubbert, and R.L. Spitzer, "Association of Binge Eating Disorder and Psychiatric Comorbidity in Obese Subjects," *American Journal of Psychiatry*, vol. 150, October 1993, p. 1472.

8. Ibid., Table 2, p. 1475.

9. This analysis draws on the paper by F. McManus and G. Waller, "A Functional Analysis of Binge-Eating," *Clinical Psychology Review*, vol. 15, issue 8, 1995.

10. S.F. Abraham and P.J. Beaumont, "How Patients Describe Bulimia or Binge Eating," *Psychological Medicine*, vol. 12, August 1982.

11. C.G. Greeno and R.R. Wing, "Stress-induced Eating," *Psychological Bulletin*, vol. 115, May 1994, p. 451.

12. This particular analysis is presented for the first time in this book. For a description of the basic research for this technique, see P.R. Robbins and R.H. Tanck, "A Factor Analysis of Coping Behaviors," *Journal of Clinical Psychology*, vol. 34, April 1978, pp. 379–380.

13. T.F. Heatherton and R.F. Baumeister, "Binge Eating as Escape from Self-Awareness," *Psychological Bulletin*, vol. 110, July 1991, p. 95.

Chapter 6. Treatment of Eating Disorders

1. "Eating Disorders," (Rockville, Md.: National Institute of Mental Health, 1993), p. 12.

2. A.E. Anderson, "Inpatient and Outpatient Treatment of Anorexia Nervosa," in K.D. Brownell and J.P. Foreyt (eds.), *Handbook of Eating Disorders: Physiology, Psychology, and Treatment of Obesity, Anorexia, and Bulimia* (New York: Basic Books, 1986), p. 336.

3. A.B. Middleman, H.J. Binns, and R.H. Durant, "Factors Affecting Pediatric Residents' Intentions to Screen for High Risk Behaviors," *Journal of Adolescent Health*, vol. 17, August 1995, p. 110.

4. P.S. Mehler, "Eating Disorders: 1. Anorexia Nervosa," *Hospital Practice*, January 15, 1996, pp. 111–112.

5. R.C. Casper and L.N. Jabine, "An Eight-Year Follow-Up: Outcome from Adolescent Compared to Adult Onset Anorexia Nervosa," *Journal of Youth and Adolescence*, vol. 25, August 1996, p. 499.

6. American Psychiatric Association, "Practice Guideline for Eating Disorders," *American Journal of Psychiatry*, vol. 150, February 1993, p. 216.

7. Ibid., p. 217.

8. W.S. Agras, J.A. Schneider, B. Arnow, S.D. Raeburn, and C.F. Telch, "Cognitive-Behavioral and Response-Prevention Treatments for Bulimia Nervosa," *Journal of Consulting and Clinical Psychology*, vol. 57, April 1989, p. 220.

9. Ibid., p. 215.

10. Agras et al., pp. 218–219.

11. C. Johnson, M.E. Connors, and D.L. Tobin, "Symptom Management of Bulimia," *Journal of Consulting and Clinical Psychology*, vol. 55, October 1987, pp. 671–672.

12. Ibid., p. 672.

13. Ibid.

14. J.C. Rosen and H. Leitenberg, "Bulimia Nervosa: Treatment with Exposure and Response Prevention," *Behavior Therapy*, vol. 13, January 1982.

15. See, for example, M.D. Marcus, R.R. Wing, and J. Hopkins, "Obese Binge Eaters: Affect, Cognitions, and Response to Behavioral Weight Control," *Journal of Consulting and Clinical Psychology*, vol. 56, June 1988, p. 435.

16. S.V. Owen and M.L. Fullerton, "Would It Make a Difference? A Discussion Group in a Behaviorally Oriented Inpatient Eating Disorder Program," *Journal of Psychosocial Nursing*, vol. 33, November 1995, p. 36.

Chapter 7. Society and Eating Disorders

1. R.J. Freedman, *Beauty Bound* (Lexington, Mass.: Lexington Books, 1986), p. 150.

2. D.M. Garner, P.E. Garfinkel, D. Schwartz, and M. Thompson, "Culture Expectations of Thinness in Women," Psychological Reports, vol. 47, October 1980, p. 483.

3. W. Shakespeare, *Julius Caesar*, Act 1, Scene 2.

4. L.W. Banner, *American Beauty* (New York: Knopf, 1983), p. 106.

5. Ibid., p. 45

6. D.A. Zellner, D.E. Harner, and R.L. Adler, "Effects of Eating Abnormalities and Gender on Perceptions of Desirable Body Shape," *Journal of Abnormal Psychology*, vol. 98, February 1989, p. 94.

7. Ibid., p. 94.

8. Ibid.

9. G.W. Guyot, L. Fairchild, and M. Hill, "Physical Fitness, Sport Participation, Body Build and Self-Concept of Elementary School Children," *International Journal of Sport Psychology*, vol. 12, issue 2, 1981, pp. 112–113.

10. S.A. French, C.L. Perry, G.R. Leon, and J.A. Fulkerson, "Dieting Behaviors and Weight Change History in Female Adolescents," *Health Psychology*, vol. 14, November 1995, p. 548.

11. R.M. Raich, J.C. Rosen, J. Degs, O. Perez, A. Requena, and J. Gross, "Eating Disorder Symptoms among Adolescents in the United States and Spain: A Comparative Study," *International Journal of Eating Disorders*, vol. 11, January 1992.

12. D.M. Buss, "Sex Differences in Human Male Preferences: Evolutionary Hypotheses Tested in 37 Cultures," *Behavioral and Brain Sciences*, vol. 12, March 1989.

13. R.H. Striegel-Moore, L.R. Silberstein, and J. Rodin, "Toward an Understanding of Risk Factors for Bulimia," *American Psychologist*, vol. 41, March 1986, p. 249.

14. Ibid.

15. H. Lytton and D.M. Romney, "Parents' Differential Socialization of Boys and Girls: A Meta-Analysis," *Psychological Bulletin*, vol. 109, March 1991, pp. 286–287.

16. M.G. Weiss, "Eating Disorders and Disordered Eating in Different Cultures," *Cultural Psychiatry*, vol. 18, September 1995.

Chapter 8. Prevention of Eating Disorders

1. C.M. Shisslak, M. Crago, M.E. Neal, and B. Swain, "Primary Prevention of Eating Disorders," *Journal of Consulting and Clinical Psychology*, vol. 55, October 1987, p. 663.

2. Ibid., p. 664.

3. G.R. Leon, J.A. Fulkerson, C.I. Perry, and A. Dube, "Family Influences, School Behaviors, and Risk for the Later Development of an Eating Disorder," *Journal of Youth and Adolescence*, vol. 23, October 1994, pp. 505–506.

4. "Nutrition and Your Health: Dietary Guidelines for Americans," fourth edition (Washington, D.C.: U.S. Department of Agriculture, 1995), p. 5.

5. G.A. Bray, ed., *Obesity in Perspective, A Conference*, Bethesda, Md.: National Institutes of Health, 1975. The tables were adapted from the table of the Metropolitan Life Insurance Company.

6. Ibid.

7. S.A. French, C.L. Perry, G.R. Leon, and J.A. Fulkerson, "Dieting Behaviors and Weight Change History in Female Adolescents," *Health Psychology*, vol. 14, November 1995, Table 1, p. 549.

8. Ibid., p. 554.

9. "Woman's Health Research Institute Begins Study on Eating Disorder," *Woman's Quarterly*, Spring 1996.

10. Leon et al.

Glossary

anorexia nervosa—An eating disorder in which people intentionally starve themselves.

antidepressant medicines—Drugs that are effective for many people in diminishing the symptoms of depression.

binge eating disorder—An eating disorder in which people eat large amounts of food and do so without a feeling of control over what they are doing.

body image—The perception one has of one's own body.

bulimia nervosa—An eating disorder in which people eat large amounts of food and then try to get rid of it by vomiting, by using laxatives or diuretics, or by fasting or exercising excessively.

cognitive-behavioral therapy—A technique of psychotherapy that tries to change patients' negative views of themselves, their environments, and their future, as well as their ineffective and self-defeating behaviors.

cognitive dissonance—Psychological conflict resulting from a difference between one's attitudes and behavior. The theory of cognitive dissonance holds that there is a tendency for a person's attitude to become consistent with his or her behavior.

cultural lag—A situation that arises when there are changes in some aspects of a culture while other aspects remain unchanged.

culture—The shared experiences, values, beliefs, and traditions of a people.

depression—A group of symptoms such as a feeling of sadness, poor sleep, inability to concentrate, and loss of interest in usual activities that persist over time.

diuretics—Medications that increase elimination of fluid from the body.

fasting girls—Girls in the 1700s and 1800s who were said to eat nothing or next to nothing yet somehow survived.

obesity—Being considerably overweight, at least 20 percent higher than the upper limit indicated in height–weight tables.

obsessive-compulsive disorder—A psychiatric disorder in which people experience obsessions (recurrent thoughts that seem to invade their consciousness) or compulsions (repetitive behaviors such as hand washing or compulsive checking).

refeeding—The process of gradually introducing normal amounts of food to people who have been starving.

serotonin—A chemical that plays a role in the transmission of messages within the brain and through the nervous system.

stereotypes—Views that people hold about groups of people such as people of a particular race, religion, or nationality. Stereotypes are also held about people who are obese.

sulci—Fissures, chiefly of the brain.

Further Reading

Brownell, Kelly D., and Foreyt, John P. (eds.). *Handbook of Eating Disorders: Physiology, Psychology, and Treatment of Obesity, Anorexia, and Bulimia.* New York: Basic Books, 1986.

Bruch, Hilde. *The Golden Cage: The Enigma of Anorexia Nervosa.* Cambridge, Mass.: Harvard University Press, 1978.

Brumberg, Joan J. *Fasting Girls: The Emergence of Anorexia Nervosa as a Modern Disease.* Cambridge, Mass.: Harvard University Press, 1988.

Centers for Disease Control and Prevention, "Guidelines for School Health Programs to Promote Lifelong Healthy Eating," *Morbidity and Mortality Weekly Report,* 45, June 14, 1996.

Crisfiel, Deborah. *Eating Disorders.* Parsippany, N.J.: Silver Burdett Press, 1994.

"Eating Disorders." Rockville, Md.: National Institute of Mental Health, 1993.

Erlanger, Ellen. *Eating Disorders: A Question & Answer Book about Anorexia Nervosa & Bulimia Nervosa.* Minneapolis: The Lerner Publishing Group, 1988.

Fairburn, Christopher G. *Overcoming Binge Eating.* New York: Guilford Press, 1995.

Kolodny, Nancy J. *When Food's a Foe: How to Confront and Conquer Eating Disorders.* Boston: Little, Brown,& Co., 1992.

Levine, Michael P. *How Schools Can Help Combat Student Eating Disorders: Anorexia Nervosa and Bulimia.* Washington, D.C.: National Education Association, 1987.

"Nutrition and Your Health: Dietary Guidelines for Americans." Fourth edition. Washington, D.C.: U.S. Department of Agriculture, 1995.

Sonder, Ben. *When Food Turns Against You.* New York: Franklin Watts, Inc., 1993.

Wolhart, Dayna. *Anorexia & Bulimia.* Parsippany, N.J.: Silver Burdett Press, 1988.

Index